EDMOND ROSTAND

CYRANO DE BERGERAC
Heroic Comedy in Five Acts

Buccaneer Books
Cutchogue, New York

It was to Cyrano's soul that I intended to dedicate this poem.

But since his soul has passed into you, Coquelin,* I dedicate it to you.

E. R.

---

* Benoît-Constant Coquelin (1841–1909) was the French actor who played the part of Cyrano when the play opened in 1897. (All footnotes are by the translator.)

Contents

ACT ONE: A Performance at the Hôtel de
  Bourgogne   11
ACT TWO: The Poets' Cookshop   58
ACT THREE: Roxane's Kiss   100
ACT FOUR: The Gascon Cadets   141
ACT FIVE: Cyrano's Gazette   185

Dramatis Personae

Cyrano de Bergerac
Christian de Neuvillette
Count de Guiche
Ragueneau
Le Bret
Carbon de Castel-Jaloux
The Cadets
Lignière
Viscount de Valvert
A Marquis
Second Marquis
Third Marquis
Montfleury
Bellerose
Jodelet
Cuigy
D'Artagnan
Brissaille
A Meddler
A Musketeer
Second Musketeer
A Spanish Officer
A Light-Horseman
The Doorkeeper
A Burgher
A Thief
A Spectator
A Guardsman
Bertrandou the Fifer
The Capuchin
Two Musicians
Poets
Pastry Cooks

Roxane
Sister Marthe
Lise
The Refreshment Girl
Mother Marguerite de Jésus
The Duenna
Sister Claire
An Actress
The Soubrette
Pages
The Flower Girl
A Lady
A Lady Intellectual
A Nun

Crowd, Burghers, Marquis, Musketeers, Thieves, Pastry Cooks, Poets, Cadets, Gascons, Actors, Violinists, Pages, Children, Spanish Soldiers, Spectators, Lady Intellectuals, Actresses, Nuns, etc.

The first four acts are set in 1640, the fifth in 1655.

ACT ONE

A Performance at the Hôtel de Bourgogne*

The auditorium of the Hôtel de Bourgogne in 1640. It resembles an indoor tennis court, decorated and fitted out for theatrical performances.

It is a long rectangle, seen diagonally, so that one side forms the background, extending from downstage right to upstage left, where it forms an angle with the stage, which is seen obliquely.

There are benches on both sides of this stage. The curtain consists of two tapestries that can be drawn apart. Above the proscenium, the royal arms. Broad steps from the stage to the floor of the auditorium. Places for musicians on both sides of these steps. A row of candles for footlights.

The top section of the gallery on one side is divided into boxes. No seats in the front of the auditorium, whose floor is the stage of the actual theater. At the back—that is, downstage right—are benches arranged in tiers. A staircase leads to the upper seats; only its

* A theater whose full name was the Théâtre de l'Hôtel de Bourgogne, the word *hôtel* being used here with its old meaning of "mansion" or "town house." The Hôtel de Bourgogne was the Paris residence of the Dukes of Burgundy (Bourgogne) in the fourteenth and fifteenth centuries. In 1548, when it had been partially demolished, a theater was built on its site and named after the original building.

11

lower part is visible. Under it is a refreshment table adorned with little candelabra, vases of flowers, crystal goblets, plates of pastry, bottles, etc.

Upstage center, under the boxes, is the entrance to the auditorium, a big double door partially opened to admit the audience. On the panels of this door, as well as in several corners and above the refreshment table, are red posters bearing the name of the play: La Clorise.

As the curtain rises, the auditorium is in semidarkness, and still empty. The chandeliers have been lowered to the middle of the floor and are waiting to be lighted.

Scene I

The Audience, arriving little by little. Cavaliers, Burghers, Lackeys, Pages, Thieves, the Doorkeeper, etc., then the Marquis, Cuigy, Brissaille, the Refreshment Girl, the Violinists, etc.

(*A tumult of voices is heard from outside the door, then a* CAVALIER *enters abruptly.*)

THE DOORKEEPER
(*Pursuing him*)
Stop! You haven't paid your fifteen sols!

THE CAVALIER
I don't have to pay!

THE DOORKEEPER
Why not?

THE CAVALIER
I'm a light-horseman of the King's Household.

THE DOORKEEPER
(*To another* CAVALIER *who has just entered*)
And you?

SECOND CAVALIER
I don't have to pay either.

THE DOORKEEPER
But . . .

SECOND CAVALIER
I'm a musketeer.

FIRST CAVALIER
(*To the second*)
The play doesn't begin till two o'clock and the floor is
empty. Let's have a little fencing practice.
(*They fence with the foils they have brought.*)

A LACKEY
(*Entering*)
Psst! ... Flanquin! ...

SECOND LACKEY
(*Who has already arrived*)
Yes, Champagne?

FIRST LACKEY
(*Showing him what he takes out of his doublet*)
Look: I have cards and dice. (*Sits down on the floor.*) Let's
play.

SECOND LACKEY
(*Also sitting down*)
Good idea, my friend.

FIRST LACKEY
(*Takes a candle stub from his pocket, lights it, and sets
it on the floor.*)
I've stolen a little light from my master.

A GUARDSMAN
(*To a* FLOWER GIRL *coming toward him*)
It's nice of you to come before the lights are lit!
(*Takes hold of her waist.*)

ONE OF THE FENCERS
(*Receiving a thrust of his opponent's foil*)
Touché!

ONE OF THE CARD PLAYERS
A club!

THE GUARDSMAN
(*Pursuing the* FLOWER GIRL)
A kiss!

THE FLOWER GIRL
(*Pushing him away*)
They'll see us!

THE GUARDSMAN
(*Pulling her into a dark corner*)
No danger of that!

A MAN
(*Sitting down on the floor with others who have brought food*)
When you come early, you can eat in comfort.

A BURGHER
(*Leading his son*)
Let's sit here, my son.

A CARD PLAYER
Three aces!

ANOTHER MAN
(*Taking a bottle from under his cloak and sitting down*)
A drunk should drink his Burgundy . . . (*Drinks.*) . . . in
the House of Burgundy!

THE BURGHER
(*To his son*)
It's as if we were in some den of evil! (*Points to the drunk-ard with his cane.*) Drinkers! (*In stepping back, one of the fencers jostles him.*) Brawlers! (*He falls in the midst of the card players.*) Gamblers!

THE GUARDSMAN
(*Behind him, still grappling with the* FLOWER GIRL)
A kiss!

THE BURGHER
(*Hurriedly leading his son away*)
Good heavens! To think that Rotrou* was performed in
such a place as this, my son!

THE YOUNG MAN
And Corneille!

A BAND OF PAGES
(*They enter holding hands, dancing, and singing.*)
Tra-la-la-la-la-la-la-la-la-la-la . . .

THE DOORKEEPER
(*Sternly, to the* PAGES)
Behave yourselves, boys! No pranks!

FIRST PAGE
(*With wounded dignity*)
Oh, sir, how can you even suspect such a thing? (*With ani-mation, to the* SECOND PAGE, *as soon as the* DOORKEEPER *has turned his back*) Do you have your string?

* Jean de Rotrou (1609–1650), French playwright.

SECOND PAGE

Yes, and my fishhook.

FIRST PAGE

Good. We'll fish for wigs when we're up there.

A THIEF

(*Gathering several disreputable-looking men around him*)

Come closer, my young rascals, and let me educate you. Since you're about to try your hand at stealing for the first time . . .

SECOND PAGE

(*Shouting to other* PAGES *in the upper gallery*)

Hey! Have you brought your peashooters?

THIRD PAGE

Yes! And peas, too!
(*Blows peas at them.*)

THE YOUNG MAN

(*To his father*)

What's the name of the play?

THE BURGHER

La Clorise.

THE YOUNG MAN

Who wrote it?

THE BURGHER

Monsieur Balthazar Baro.* It's a play that . . .
(*Walks upstage, holding his son's arm.*)

THE THIEF

(*To his disciples*)

. . . and lace, especially on the legs. Cut it off. . . .

A SPECTATOR

(*To another, pointing to a corner of the gallery*)

I was up there at the first performance of *The Cid.*

THE THIEF

(*Making the gesture of picking a pocket*)

Watches . . .

THE BURGHER

(*Walking downstage with his son*)

You'll see some very famous actors . . .

---

* Balthazar Baro (1600–1650) was a French playwright and novelist whose dramatic works have now faded into oblivion.

THE THIEF
(*Making the gesture of furtively and delicately pulling out a handkerchief*)
Handkerchiefs . . .

THE BURGHER
Montfleury, for example . . .

A VOICE FROM THE UPPER GALLERY
Light the chandeliers!

THE BURGHER
. . . Bellerose, L'Epy, La Beaupré, Jodelet!*

A PAGE
(*On the floor*)
Ah, here's the refreshment girl!

THE REFRESHMENT GIRL
(*Appearing behind the refreshment table*)
Oranges, milk, raspberry syrup, cider. . . .
(*Commotion at the door*)

A HIGH-PITCHED VOICE
Out of the way, you brutes!

A LACKEY
(*Surprised*)
Are there marquis down here on the floor?

ANOTHER LACKEY
Not for long.
(*A group of young* MARQUIS *enters.*)

A MARQUIS
(*Seeing that the theater is half empty*)
What's this? We've arrived like tradesmen, without disturbing people, without stepping on their feet? What a shameful way to make an entrance! (*Finds himself in front of some other noblemen who have entered shortly before.*) Cuigy! Brissaille!
(*They embrace enthusiastically.*)

CUIGY
Ah, the faithful are here! Yes, it's true: we've come before the candles. . . .

THE MARQUIS
No, don't talk about it! I'm so annoyed. . . .

* Bellerose, L'Epy, La Beaupré, and Jodelet, as well as Montfleury, mentioned above, were all French actors of the time in which the play is set.

ANOTHER MARQUIS

Cheer up, Marquis, here comes the lighter!

THE CROWD

(*Greeting the entrance of the lighter*)

Ah! . . .

(*Groups form around the chandeliers as he lights them. A few people have taken their places in the galleries.* LIGNIÈRE *and* CHRISTIAN DE NEUVILLETTE *enter, arm in arm.* LIGNIÈRE *is rather disheveled, with the face of a distinguished drunkard.* CHRISTIAN *is elegantly dressed, but in a somewhat outmoded style. He seems preoccupied, and looks up at the boxes.*)

Scene II

The same, with Christian and Lignière, then Ragueneau and Le Bret.

CUIGY

Lignière!

BRISSAILLE

(*Laughing*)

Still sober!

LIGNIÈRE

(*Aside, to* CHRISTIAN)

Shall I introduce you? (CHRISTIAN *nods.*) Baron de Neuvillette.

(*They bow.*)

THE CROWD

(*Acclaiming the raising of the first lighted chandelier*)

Ah!

CUIGY

(*To* BRISSAILLE, *looking at* CHRISTIAN)

He has a charming face!

FIRST MARQUIS

(*Disdainfully, having overheard*)

Really!

LIGNIÈRE

(*Introducing them to* CHRISTIAN)

Messieurs de Cuigy, de Brissaille. . . .

CHRISTIAN

(*Bowing*)
Delighted to meet you, gentlemen.

FIRST MARQUIS

(*To the second*)
He's rather handsome, but he's not dressed in the latest fashion.

LIGNIÈRE

(*To* CUIGY)
Monsieur de Neuvillette has just arrived from Touraine.

CHRISTIAN

Yes, I've been in Paris only three weeks. I'm entering the Guards tomorrow, as a Cadet.

FIRST MARQUIS

(*Looking at the people entering the boxes*)
There's Madame Aubry, the magistrate's wife!

THE REFRESHMENT GIRL

Oranges, milk. . . .

THE VIOLINISTS

(*Tuning their instruments*)
La . . . la . . .

CUIGY

(*To* CHRISTIAN, *pointing to the auditorium, which is beginning to fill*)
People are arriving.

CHRISTIAN

Yes, in droves!

FIRST MARQUIS

All of fashionable society is here!
(*They name the richly dressed ladies as they enter the boxes, bowing to them and receiving smiles in return.*)

SECOND MARQUIS

Mesdames de Guéméné . . .

CUIGY

De Bois-Dauphin . . .

FIRST MARQUIS

Whom we have loved . . .

BRISSAILLE

De Chavigny . . .

SECOND MARQUIS

Who plays with our hearts!

LIGNIÈRE

I see Monsieur de Corneille has come from Rouen.

THE YOUNG MAN

(*To his father*)
Is the Academy* here?

THE BURGHER

I see several members. There's Boudu, and Boissat, and Cureau de la Chambre; Porchères, Colomby, Bourzeys, Bourdon, Arbaud. . . . All those names that will never die! It's awesome to see such men!

FIRST MARQUIS

Look, our lady intellectuals are taking their places: Barthénoïde, Urimédonte, Cassandace, Félixérie. . . .

SECOND MARQUIS

(*Ecstatically*)
Dear God, but their surnames are exquisite! Marquis, do you know them all?

FIRST MARQUIS

I know them all, Marquis!

LIGNIÈRE

(*Taking* CHRISTIAN *aside*)
My friend, I came with you to help you, but since the lady isn't here I'll return to my vice.

CHRISTIAN

(*Imploringly*)
No, stay! You know everyone at court and in the city: you'll be able to tell me the name of the lady for whom I'm dying of love.

THE FIRST VIOLINIST

(*Rapping on his desk with his bow*)
Ready, gentlemen. . . .
(*Raises his bow.*)

THE REFRESHMENT GIRL

Macaroons, lemonade. . . .
(*The violins begin playing.*)

CHRISTIAN

I'm afraid she may be coquettish and refined. I don't dare to speak to her, because I have no wit. I don't know how to

* The French Academy, founded in 1635 and still in existence. Its membership is limited to forty of the most distinguished French writers. The men named below (Boudu, Boissat, etc.) were among its earlier members.

use the elegant language that's in style nowadays. I'm only a soldier, a shy soldier. . . . She always sits in that box—there, on the right. It's still empty. . . .

LIGNIÈRE
(Preparing to leave)
I'm going.

CHRISTIAN
(Holding him back)
Oh, no! Stay!

LIGNIÈRE
I can't. D'Assoucy is waiting for me at the tavern. A man could die of thirst here!

THE REFRESHMENT GIRL
(Passing in front of him with a tray)
Orangeade?

LIGNIÈRE
Bah!

THE REFRESHMENT GIRL
Milk?

LIGNIÈRE
Are you trying to make me sick?

THE REFRESHMENT GIRL
White wine?

LIGNIÈRE
Aha! (*To* CHRISTIAN) I'll stay a little longer, since you insist. (*To the* REFRESHMENT GIRL) Now, about that white wine. . . .
(He sits down near the refreshment table and she pours him a glass of wine.)

VOICES FROM THE CROWD
(Greeting the entrance of a plump, jolly-looking little man)
Ah, Ragueneau!

LIGNIÈRE
(To CHRISTIAN)
There's Ragueneau, the great baker.

RAGUENEAU
(Dressed like a pastry cook in his Sunday best, hurrying toward LIGNIÈRE)
Sir, have you seen Monsieur de Cyrano?

LIGNIÈRE
(*Introducing* RAGUENEAU *to* CHRISTIAN)
This is Ragueneau, the pastry cook of actors and poets!

RAGUENEAU
(*Embarrassed*)
You honor me too highly.

LIGNIÈRE
Not at all! You're a patron of the arts!

RAGUENEAU
Poets do come to my shop . . .

LIGNIÈRE
To buy on credit. And you yourself are a talented poet.

RAGUENEAU
So I've been told.

LIGNIÈRE
You're madly in love with poetry!

RAGUENEAU
It's true that for an ode . . .

LIGNIÈRE
You give a tart.

RAGUENEAU
Only a little one, if it's a short ode.

LIGNIÈRE
No need to apologize! Such modesty! And what do you give for a triolet?

RAGUENEAU
Rolls.

LIGNIÈRE
(*Sternly*)
Rolls of the very highest quality. You love the theater, too, don't you?

RAGUENEAU
I adore it.

LIGNIÈRE
You pay for your theater tickets with pastry! Tell me, just between ourselves, how much did you pay this time?

RAGUENEAU
Four custard tarts and fifteen cream puffs. (*Looks all around.*) Monsieur de Cyrano isn't here? I'm surprised.

LIGNIÈRE

Why?

RAGUENEAU

Montfleury is in the play!

LIGNIÈRE

Yes, that walking barrel will play the part of Phaedo today.
But what does it matter to Cyrano?

RAGUENEAU

Haven't you heard? He took a dislike to Montfleury and
ordered him not to appear on the stage for a month.

LIGNIÈRE
(Who has by now taken his fourth glass of wine)
Well, what of it?

RAGUENEAU

Montfleury is in the play!

CUIGY
(Who has joined the group)
There's nothing he can do about it.

RAGUENEAU

Ah, that's what I've come to see!

FIRST MARQUIS

Who is this Cyrano?

CUIGY

He's a man who knows how to handle a rapier.

SECOND MARQUIS

A nobleman?

CUIGY

Noble enough. He's a Cadet* in the Guards. *(Points to a
gentleman who is walking back and forth as though looking
for someone.)* But his friend Le Bret can tell you. . . .
(Calls him.) Le Bret! (LE BRET *comes over to them.*)
You're looking for Bergerac?

LE BRET

Yes, and I'm worried. . . .

CUIGY

He's an extraordinary man, isn't he?

* In seventeenth-century France, a Cadet was a nobleman serving
as a common soldier or noncommissioned officer in order to acquire
military experience and knowledge that he would later use as an
officer.

LE BRET

(*Affectionately*)
The most delightful man under the sun!

RAGUENEAU

A poet!

CUIGY

A swordsman!

BRISSAILLE

A scientist!

LE BRET

A musician!

LIGNIÈRE

And what an uncommon appearance!

RAGUENEAU

Yes, I doubt that the solemn Philippe de Champaigne will ever paint him for us. But odd, impetuous, brash, and outlandish as he is, proudest of all the thin-skinned swaggerers lovingly spawned by Gascony, I think he would have given the late Jacques Callot a wild swashbuckler to place among his portraits. With his triple-plumed hat, his billowing doublet, and his cape majestically held out behind by a sword that rises like the insolent tail of a cock, he carries his nose above a punchinello ruff, a nose that . . . Ah, gentlemen, what a nose! Those who see it pass by can't help exclaiming, "No, it can't be true!" Then they smile and say, "He'll soon take it off." But Monsieur de Bergerac never takes it off.

LE BRET

(*Nodding*)
He keeps it on—and runs his sword through anyone who looks at it too closely.

RAGUENEAU

(*Proudly*)
His blade is half the shears of Fate!

FIRST MARQUIS

(*Shrugging*)
He won't come.

RAGUENEAU

He will! I'll bet you a chicken à la Ragueneau!

FIRST MARQUIS

(*Laughing*)
I'll take that bet!

(*Murmurs of admiration from the crowd:* ROXANE *has just appeared in her box. She sits at the front of it, her* DUENNA *sits at the rear.* CHRISTIAN, *occupied in paying the* REFRESHMENT GIRL, *has not yet seen her.*)

SECOND MARQUIS
(*With little cries*)
Gentlemen, she's terrifyingly lovely!

FIRST MARQUIS
Skin like a peach, smiling with strawberry lips!

SECOND MARQUIS
And so fresh and cool that anyone coming near her might catch a cold in his heart!

CHRISTIAN
(*Looks up, sees* ROXANE, *and clutches* LIGNIÈRE'*s arm.*)
There she is!

LIGNIÈRE
(*Looking*)
Ah, so she's the one?

CHRISTIAN
Yes. Quickly, tell me who she is! I'm afraid.

LIGNIÈRE
(*Still sipping his wine*)
Magdeleine Robin, known as Roxane. Sharp-witted, an intellectual . . .

CHRISTIAN
Alas!

LIGNIÈRE
. . . free, an orphan, a cousin of Cyrano, whom we were just discussing. . . .
(*At this point a very elegant gentleman, wearing the Cordon Bleu around his neck, enters* ROXANE'*s box and stands talking with her for a few moments.*)

CHRISTIAN
(*Starting*)
Who is that man?

LIGNIÈRE
(*Winking, beginning to show the effects of the wine*)
That, my friend, is Count de Guiche. He's in love with her, but he's married to Cardinal Richelieu's niece. He wants to

arrange a marriage between Roxane and Viscount de Valvert, a sad specimen of a man whom he can count on to
be obliging. She's opposed to it, but De Guiche is powerful:
he can persecute an untitled girl like her. Incidentally, I've
written a song exposing his crafty scheme. He must hate me
for it! The ending is positively vicious. Listen, I'll sing it
for you. . . .
(*He rises unsteadily to his feet and holds up his glass,
ready to sing.*)

CHRISTIAN

No. I'm leaving now.

LIGNIÈRE

Where are you going?

CHRISTIAN

I'm going to pay a visit to Viscount de Valvert!

LIGNIÈRE

Don't do anything rash: there's a good chance he'd kill
you. (*Discreetly calls his attention to* ROXANE.) Stay.
You're being watched.

CHRISTIAN

It's true!
(*He stands staring at her. Seeing him looking up with
his mouth open, the* THIEF *and his accomplices begin
moving toward him.*)

LIGNIÈRE

I'm the one who's leaving. I'm thirsty and I have an appointment—in a tavern!
(*He staggers out.*)

LE BRET

(*With relief, coming back to* RAGUENEAU *after having
searched everywhere*)
No sign of Cyrano.

RAGUENEAU

(*Incredulously*)
It doesn't seem possible.

LE BRET

I'm hoping he hasn't seen the poster.

THE CROWD

Begin the play! Begin!

Scene III

The same, except for Lignière; De Guiche, Valvert, then Montfleury.

A MARQUIS
(*Watching* DE GUICHE *come down from* ROXANE's *box and walk across the floor, surrounded by obsequious noblemen, one of whom is* VISCOUNT DE VALVERT)
De Guiche has his own little court!

SECOND MARQUIS
(*With distaste*)
Another Gascon!

FIRST MARQUIS
Yes, but a flexible, calculating Gascon—the kind who succeeds! We'd better go and pay our respects to him, take my word for it.
(*They approach* DE GUICHE.)

SECOND MARQUIS
What beautiful ribbons, Monsieur de Guiche! What would you call that color? Is it "Kiss-me-my-darling," or is it "Doe's-belly?"

DE GUICHE
I call it "Sick Spaniard."

FIRST MARQUIS
An appropriate name, because soon, thanks to your valor, the Spaniards in Flanders* will be in very sickly condition!

DE GUICHE
I'm going to sit on the stage. Are you coming with me? (*He walks toward the stage, followed by all the* MARQUIS *and other noblemen, then looks back and calls.*) Come, Valvert!
(CHRISTIAN *has been observing and listening to them. He starts when he hears* VALVERT's *name.*)

CHRISTIAN
Valvert! I'll throw my glove in his face this instant! (*Reaches for his gloves and encounters the hand of a thief picking his pocket. Turns around.*) What . . .

* At the time of the play the French were fighting the Spanish for possession of Flanders, then part of the Spanish Netherlands.

26

THE THIEF

Oh, no!

CHRISTIAN

(*Holding him*)
I was reaching for a glove!

THE THIEF

(*With a pitiful smile*)
You found a hand instead. (*Lowering his voice and speaking rapidly*) Let me go and I'll tell you a secret.

CHRISTIAN

(*Still holding him*)
What is it?

THE THIEF

Lignière, who just left you . . .

CHRISTIAN

(*Without letting go of him*)
Yes? Go on.

THE THIEF

He's about to meet his death. He wrote a song that offended a certain very powerful person, and tonight a hundred men—I know, because I'm to join them soon—have been posted . . .

CHRISTIAN

A hundred! By whom?

THE THIEF

Sorry, I can't tell you that.

CHRISTIAN

(*Shrugging*)
Oh, come, come!

THE THIEF

(*With great dignity*)
It's a professional secret!

CHRISTIAN

Where are the men posted?

THE THIEF

At the Porte de Nesle, on his way. Warn him!

CHRISTIAN

(*Finally letting go of him*)
But how can I find him?

THE THIEF

Hurry to all his favorite taverns—the Golden Winepress, the Pine Cone, the Breaking Belt, the Two Torches, the Three Funnels—and leave a note for him in each of them.

CHRISTIAN

Yes, I'll go! Oh, the vile cowards! A hundred men against one! (*Looks at* ROXANE *with love.*) How can I bear to leave her? (*At* VALVERT *with fury*) And him! But I must save Lignière!

(*He runs out.* DE GUICHE, VALVERT, *the* MARQUIS, *and the other noblemen have disappeared behind the curtain to take their places on the benches on the stage. The floor, the gallery, and the boxes are now completely filled.*)

THE CROWD

Begin the play!

A BURGHER

(*Whose wig has just been hooked and lifted at the end of a string by a* PAGE *in the upper gallery*)
My wig!

JOYOUS SHOUTS

He's bald!—Good work, page!—Ha! ha! ha!

THE BURGHER

(*Angrily shaking his fist*)
You young bandit!

LAUGHTER AND SHOUTS

(*Beginning loudly, then dying away*)
Ha! ha! ha! ha! ha! ha!
(*Complete silence*)

LE BRET

(*Astonished*)
Why this sudden silence? (*A* SPECTATOR *speaks to him in an undertone.*) Oh?

THE SPECTATOR

Yes, it was just told to me by someone who knows for certain.

MURMURS

(*All through the crowd*)
Sh!—Is it true?—No!—Yes!—In the grilled box.—The Cardinal!—The Cardinal?—The Cardinal!

A PAGE

That means the end of all our fun!

(*Three raps are heard from the stage. Everyone becomes motionless and waits.*)

THE VOICE OF A MARQUIS
(*In the silence, from behind the curtain*)
Put out that candle!

ANOTHER MARQUIS
(*Putting his head between the two halves of the curtain*)
A chair!
(*A chair is passed from hand to hand, above the heads of the audience. The* MARQUIS *takes it and disappears, after throwing a few kisses to the boxes.*)

A SPECTATOR
Silence!
(*Three more raps from the stage. The curtain opens. Tableau. The* MARQUIS *are seated on either side of the stage in insolent poses. The backdrop represents a bluish pastoral scene. Four small crystal chandeliers light the stage. The violins are playing softly.*)

LE BRET
(*To* RAGUENEAU, *in a low voice*)
Will Montfleury soon be on the stage?

RAGUENEAU
(*Also in a low voice*)
He'll be the first to appear.

LE BRET
Cyrano isn't here.

RAGUENEAU
I've lost my bet.

LE BRET
So much the better!
(*A bagpipe melody is heard, then the enormously fat* MONTFLEURY *appears on the stage, wearing a shepherd's costume, a hat adorned with roses tilted over one ear, blowing into a beribboned bagpipe.*)

THE CROWD
(*Applauding*)
Montfleury!—Bravo!—Montfleury!

MONTFLEURY
(*After bowing, playing the part of Phaedo*)
"Happy is he who shuns the pomp of courts
In solitary exile, self-imposed;
And who, when gentle breezes . . ."

A VOICE
(From the middle of the floor)
Haven't I ordered you off the stage for a month, you
wretched scoundrel?
*(Astonishment in the audience. Everyone looks around.
Murmurs.)*

VARIOUS VOICES
Oh!—What!—Who?
(Those in the boxes stand up to see.)

CUIGY
He's here!

LE BRET
(Terrified)
Cyrano!

THE VOICE
Off the stage this instant, king of buffoons!

THE WHOLE AUDIENCE
(Indignantly)
Oh!

MONTFLEURY
But ...

THE VOICE
You refuse?

VARIOUS VOICES
(From the floor and the boxes)
Sh!—Enough!—Go on, Montfleury!—Don't be afraid!

MONTFLEURY
(In a faltering voice)
"Happy is he who shuns the pomp of ..."

THE VOICE
(More threateningly)
Well, prince of louts, must I give your shoulders a taste
of wood?
*(An arm holding a cane rises above the heads of the
audience.)*

MONTFLEURY
(In an increasingly feeble voice)
"Happy is he who ..."
(The arm waves the cane.)

THE VOICE
Off the stage!

THE CROWD

Oh!

MONTFLEURY

(*Choking*)
"Happy is he who shuns . . ."

CYRANO

(*Standing up on a chair with his arms folded, his hat cocked, his mustache bristling, and his nose pointing aggressively*)
I'm about to lose my temper!
(*His appearance creates a sensation.*)

Scene IV

The same, with Cyrano, then Bellerose and Jodelet.

MONTFLEURY

(*To the* MARQUIS)
Protect me, gentlemen!

A MARQUIS

(*Nonchalantly*)
Go on with your acting.

CYRANO

If you do, you fat oaf, I'll tan your cheeks!

THE MARQUIS

Enough!

CYRANO

(*To all the* MARQUIS)
I advise you all to sit quietly in your seats. Otherwise my cane will rumple your ribbons!

ALL THE MARQUIS

(*Standing*)
This is too much!—Montfleury . . .

CYRANO

Montfleury will leave, if he doesn't want his ears clipped and his belly slit open!

A VOICE

But . . .

CYRANO

He will leave!

ANOTHER VOICE

You can't ...

CYRANO

Still there? (*Makes the gesture of rolling up his sleeves.*)
Very well, then, I'll go up on the stage and carve that thick
sausage into thin slices.

MONTFLEURY
(*Gathering all his dignity*)
In insulting me, sir, you insult the Dramatic Muse!

CYRANO

You are a stranger to that Muse, sir, but if she ever had the
honor of meeting you, the sight of your fat, stupid face
would inspire her to give you a vigorous kick in the broad-
est part of your anatomy!

THE CROWD

Montfleury!—Montfleury!—Baro's play!

CYRANO
(*To those shouting around him*)
Please have pity on my sword: if you don't stop shouting
you'll frighten it out of its scabbard.
(*The circle widens.*)

THE CROWD
(*Retreating*)
Make room!—Step back!

CYRANO
(*To* MONTFLEURY)
Off the stage! (*The crowd closes in with an angry murmur.
He quickly turns around.*) Is there something you want to
say to me? Speak up!
(*The crowd retreats again.*)

A VOICE
(*Singing from the back of the room*)
Monsieur de Cyrano
Is arrogant today;
His tyranny must go:
We've come to see the play!

THE WHOLE AUDIENCE
(*Singing*)
The play! The play! ...

CYRANO

If I hear any more of that song, I'll break every head in
this theater!

A BURGHER

You're not Samson!

CYRANO

I can do as well as he, sir, if you'll be so kind as to lend me your jawbone.

A LADY

(*In the boxes*)
This is incredible!

A NOBLEMAN

Scandalous!

A BURGHER

Exasperating!

A PAGE

Hilarious!

THE CROWD

Montfleury!—Cyrano!

CYRANO

Silence!

THE CROWD

(*Uproariously*)
Hee-haw!—Baa!—Woof, woof!—Cock-a-doodle-doo!

CYRANO

Quiet, or I'll . . .

A PAGE

Meow!

CYRANO

I order you to be silent! And I issue a collective challenge! Come, I'll write down your names. Step forward, young heroes! You'll all have a turn, I'll give each of you a number. Now, who wants to be at the top of the list? You, sir? No? You? No? I'll dispatch the first duelist with all the honors that are his due. All of you who want to die, hold up your hands. (*Silence*) Does modesty forbid you to look at my naked sword? No names? No hands? . . . Then I'll get on with my business. (*He turns back toward the stage, where* MONTFLEURY *has been waiting in great anxiety.*) I want to see the theater cured of this boil. Otherwise . . . (*Puts his hand to his sword.*) . . . I'll lance it!

MONTFLEURY

I . . .

CYRANO

(*Descends from his chair, sits down in the middle of the circle that has formed around him, and settles himself as though at home.*)

I'm going to clap my hands three times. By the third clap, you will be gone.

THE CROWD

(*Amused*)

Ah!

CYRANO

(*Clapping his hands*)

One!

MONTFLEURY

I . . .

A VOICE

(*From the boxes*)

Stay!

THE CROWD

He'll stay—He'll go!

MONTFLEURY

Gentlemen, I believe . . .

CYRANO

Two!

MONTFLEURY

I'm sure it would be better . . .

CYRANO

Three!

(MONTFLEURY *suddenly disappears. Storm of laughter, hisses, and boos.*)

THE CROWD

Boo!—Boo!—Coward!—Come back!

CYRANO

(*Leans back in his chair, beaming, and crosses his legs.*)

Let him come back if he dares!

A BURGHER

Here's the spokesman of the troupe!

(BELLEROSE *comes forward and bows.*)

THE BOXES

Ah!—Here's Bellerose!

BELLEROSE

(Elegantly)
Noble lords . . .

THE CROWD

No! No! Jodelet!

JODELET
(In a nasal voice, stepping forward)
Miserable clods!

THE CROWD

Ah!—Ah!—Bravo!—Very good!—Bravo!

JODELET

No bravos! Our beloved bulky tragedian has had a sudden . . .

THE CROWD

He's a coward!

JODELET

He had to leave!

THE CROWD

Call him back!

SEVERAL VOICES

No!

OTHER VOICES

Yes!

A YOUNG MAN
(To CYRANO)
Tell me, sir, what reason do you have to hate Montfleury?

CYRANO
(Graciously, still seated)
I have two reasons, my callow young friend, either of
which would be sufficient. The first is that he's a deplorable
actor who brays like an ass and wrestles ponderously with
lines that ought to soar lightly from his lips. The second—
is my secret.

THE OLD BURGHER
(Behind him)
But you're high-handedly depriving us of *La Clorise!* I
insist . . .

CYRANO
(Respectfully, turning his chair toward the BURGHER)
Sir, your pigheadedness can't change the fact that old
Baro's verse is worthless. I feel no remorse at having de-
prived you of trash.

THE LADY INTELLECTUALS

(*In the boxes*)

Oh!—Our Baro!—My dear, it's . . . How dare he!—Such insolence!

CYRANO

(*Gallantly, turning his chair toward the boxes*)

Fair ladies, blossom and be radiant, fill our dreams with longing, soften death with a smile, inspire poetry—but don't judge it!

BELLEROSE

What about the money that will have to be refunded?

CYRANO

(*Turning his chair toward the stage*)

Now there's the first sensible thing that's yet been said! Far be it from me to impose hardship on practitioners of the Thespian art. (*Stands up and throws a bag onto the stage.*) Here, take this purse and be quiet.

THE CROWD

(*Astonished*)

Ah!—Oh!

JODELET

(*Quickly picking up the purse and weighing it in his hand*)

At this price, sir, I'll be glad to have you come and stop our performance every day!

THE CROWD

Boo! Boo!

JODELET

Even if we must all be booed together!

BELLEROSE

Please clear the hall!

JODELET

Everyone out, please!

(*The spectators begin leaving while* CYRANO *watches with satisfaction, but they soon stop when they hear the following scene. The ladies in the boxes, who have already stood up and put on their cloaks, stop to listen, and finally sit down again.*)

LE BRET

(*To* CYRANO)

This is madness!

A MEDDLER

(*Who has approached* CYRANO)

What a scandal! Montfleury, the great actor! Don't you know he's protected by the Duke de Candale? Do you have a patron?

CYRANO

No!

THE MEDDLER

You don't have a ...

CYRANO

No!

THE MEDDLER

What? You have no great lord whose name protects ...

CYRANO

(*Annoyed*)

For the third time, no! Must I say it a fourth? I don't rely on some remote patron for protection. (*Puts his hand to his sword.*) My protector is always near at hand.

THE MEDDLER

Are you going to leave the city?

CYRANO

That depends.

THE MEDDLER

But the Duke de Candale has a long arm!

CYRANO

Not as long as mine ... (*Pointing to his sword*) ... when I give it this extension!

THE MEDDLER

But surely you wouldn't dare ...

CYRANO

I would.

THE MEDDLER

But ...

CYRANO

Go now.

THE MEDDLER

But ...

CYRANO

Go! Or tell me why you're looking at my nose.

THE MEDDLER
(Petrified)
I . . .

CYRANO
(Moving toward him)
Do you find it surprising?

THE MEDDLER
(Stepping back)
You're mistaken, my lord. . . .

CYRANO
Is it limp and dangling, like an elephant's trunk?

THE MEDDLER
(Stepping back again)
I didn't . . .

CYRANO
Or hooked like an owl's beak?

THE MEDDLER
I . . .

CYRANO
Do you see a wart at the end of it?

THE MEDDLER
I . . .

CYRANO
Or a fly walking on it? What's unusual about it?

THE MEDDLER
Nothing, I . . .

CYRANO
Is it a startling sight?

THE MEDDLER
Sir, I've been careful not to look at it!

CYRANO
Would you please tell me why?

THE MEDDLER
I was . . .

CYRANO
Does it disgust you?

THE MEDDLER
Sir . . .

CYRANO

Does its color seem unhealthy to you?

THE MEDDLER

Sir!

CYRANO

Is its shape obscene?

THE MEDDLER

Not at all!

CYRANO

Then why that disdainful expression? Do you find it, perhaps, a little too large?

THE MEDDLER

(*Stammering*)
Oh, no, it's quite small . . . very small . . . diminutive. . . .

CYRANO

What! How dare you accuse me of anything so ridiculous? A small nose? *My* nose? You've gone too far!

THE MEDDLER

Please, sir, I . . .

CYRANO

My nose is *enormous,* you snub-nosed, flat-faced wretch! I carry it with pride, because a big nose is a sign of affability, kindness, courtesy, wit, generosity, and courage. I have all those qualities, but you can never hope to have any of them, since the ignoble face that my hand is about to meet above your collar . . . (*Slaps him. The* MEDDLER *cries out in pain.*) . . . has no more glory, nobility, poetry, quaintness, vivacity, or grandeur—no more *nose,* in short —than the face that my boot . . . (*Turns him around by the shoulders.*) . . . is about to meet below your waist!
(*Kicks him.*)

THE MEDDLER

(*Running away*)
Help! Guards!

CYRANO

Let that be a lesson to anyone else who may feel that the middle of my face is amusing. If the joker is a nobleman, I deal with him a little differently. I administer his punishment from the front, and higher up, and not with leather, but with steel.

DE GUICHE

(Who has come down from the seats on the stage, with the MARQUIS*)*
He's beginning to be annoying!

VALVERT

(Shrugging)
He likes to bluster.

DE GUICHE

Isn't anyone going to silence him?

VALVERT

Yes, *I* will! Just watch his face when he hears what I have to say to him! *(Walks up to* CYRANO, *who observes him, and stands in front of him with a fatuous expression.)* You have a nose that . . . Your nose is . . . um . . . very big.

CYRANO

(Gravely)
Yes, very.

VALVERT

(Laughing)
Ha!

CYRANO

(With perfect calm)
Is that all?

VALVERT

Well . . .

CYRANO

I'm afraid your speech was a little short, young man. You could have said . . . oh, all sorts of things, varying your tone to fit your words. Let me give you a few examples.

In an aggressive tone: "If I had a nose like that, I'd have it amputated!"

Friendly: "The end of it must get wet when you drink from a cup. Why don't you use a tankard?"

Descriptive: "It's a rock, a peak, a cape! No, more than a cape: a peninsula!"

Curious: "What do you use that long container for? Do you keep your pens and scissors in it?"

Gracious: "What a kind man you are! You love birds so much that you've given them a perch to roost on."

Truculent: "When you light your pipe and the smoke comes out your nose, the neighbors must think a chimney has caught fire!"

Solicitous: "Be careful when you walk: with all that weight on your head, you could easily lose your balance and fall."

Thoughtful: "You ought to put an awning over it, to keep its color from fading in the sun."

Pedantic: "Sir, only the animal that Aristophanes calls the hippocampelephantocamelos could have had so much flesh and bone below its forehead."

Flippant: "That tusk must be convenient to hang your hat on."

Grandiloquent: "No wind but the mighty Arctic blast, majestic nose, could ever give you a cold from one end to the other!"

Dramatic: "When it bleeds, it must be like the Red Sea!"

Admiring: "What a sign for a perfume shop!"

Lyrical: "Is that a conch, and are you Triton risen from the sea?"

Naïve: "Is that monument open to the public?"

Respectful: "One look at your face, sir, is enough to tell me that you are indeed a man of substance."

Rustic: "That don't look like no nose to me. It's either a big cucumber or a little watermelon."

Military: "The enemy is charging! Aim your cannon!"

Practical: "A nose like that has one advantage: it keeps your feet dry in the rain."

Or finally, parodying the grief-stricken Pyramus in Théophile de Viau's play: "This nose destroyed the harmony of its good master's features! See how the traitor blushes now for shame!"*

There, now you have an inkling of what you might have said to me if you were witty and a man of letters. Unfortunately you're totally witless and a man of very few letters: only the four that spell the word "fool." But even if you had the intelligence to invent remarks like those I've given you as examples, you would not have been able to entertain me with them. You would have spoken no more than half the first syllable of the first word, because such jesting is a privilege that I grant only to myself.

DE GUICHE
(*Trying to lead away the outraged* VALVERT)
Come, never mind.

* The reference is to a line from the play *Pyrame et Thisbé* by Théophile de Viau (1590–1626): "Here is the dagger that basely sullied itself with its master's blood. It is red with shame, the traitor!"

VALVERT

(*Choking with anger*)
Such arrogance from an uncouth barbarian who . . . who
. . . isn't even wearing gloves! Who appears in public without ribbons, or tassels, or braid!

CYRANO

I have a different idea of elegance. I don't dress like a
fop, it's true, but my moral grooming is impeccable. I
never appear in public with a soiled conscience, a tarnished
honor, threadbare scruples, or an insult that I haven't
washed away. I'm always immaculately clean, adorned with
independence and frankness. I may not cut a stylish figure,
but I hold my soul erect. I wear my deeds as ribbons, my
wit is sharper than the finest mustache, and when I walk
among men I make truths ring like spurs.

VALVERT

You . . .

CYRANO

I have no gloves? It doesn't trouble me. I had a pair not
long ago, but I lost one of them, so I threw the other one
away—in someone's face.

VALVERT

Stupid lout, insolent boor, ridiculous ass!

CYRANO

(*Taking off his hat and bowing as though* VALVERT *had
just introduced himself*)
Delighted to meet you. I'm Savinien de Cyrano de Bergerac.
(*Laughter*)

VALVERT

(*Exasperated*)
Buffoon!

CYRANO

(*Crying out as if in pain*)
Oh!

VALVERT

(*Turning back, after having turned away*)
What's he saying now?

CYRANO

(*With a grimace of pain*)
I must move it: it's fallen asleep. It needs exercise. Oh!

VALVERT

What's the matter?

CYRANO

I have a cramp in my sword.

VALVERT

(*Drawing his own*)
So be it!

CYRANO

I'll give you a charming little thrust.

VALVERT

(*Contemptuously*)
Poet!

CYRANO

Yes, sir, I *am* a poet, as I'll demonstrate by composing an impromptu ballade while I fence with you.

VALVERT

A ballade?

CYRANO

You don't know what that is? Allow me to explain.

VALVERT

But . . .

CYRANO

(*As though reciting a lesson*)
The ballade consists of three eight-line stanzas . . .

VALVERT

(*Stamping his foot*)
Oh!

CYRANO

(*Continuing*)
. . . with a four-line refrain at the end.

VALVERT

You . . .

CYRANO

I'm going to compose one as I fight with you, and when I come to the last line, I'll draw blood.

VALVERT

No!

CYRANO

No? Wait and see. (*Declaiming*) "Ballade of the Duel between Monsieur de Bergerac and an Imbecile, in the Hôtel de Bourgogne."

VALVERT
What's all that?

CYRANO

It's the title.

THE CROWD
(Greatly excited)
Make room!—This will be worth seeing!—Step back!—
Quiet!
(Tableau. A circle of onlookers on the floor, with
MARQUIS *and officers mingled with* BURGHERS *and less*
affluent commoners. The PAGES *have climbed up on*
men's shoulders to see better. All the women are stand-
ing in their boxes. To the right, DE GUICHE *and his*
gentlemen; to the left, LE BRET, RAGUENEAU, CUIGY, *etc.)*

CYRANO
(Closing his eyes for a moment)
Wait, I'm thinking of how to begin. . . . There, I have it.
(His actions match his words throughout the ballade.)
I take off my hat and discard it,
I slowly abandon my cloak,
I draw my sword out of its scabbard,
Preparing to put it to use.
For the moment, I stand here before you,
Elegant, calm, and serene,
But I warn you, my impudent scoundrel,
When I end the refrain, I draw blood.

(They begin fencing.)

You should have avoided this battle.
Now, where shall I skewer you, goose?
In the side, 'neath the sleeve of your doublet?
In the heart, 'neath the ribbon you wear?
No, I've carefully thought and reflected,
And finally made up my mind;
The paunch: that's where I've decided,
When I end the refrain, to draw blood.

I see you give ground when I press you;
Your face is as white as a sheet;
Is "coward" a name that would suit you?
I dexterously parry the point
That you hoped to thrust into my entrails;
Your efforts are doomed to be vain.

Prepare yourself now to be punctured:
When I end the refrain, I draw blood.

(*Announces solemnly.*)

Refrain:
Pray God to forgive your transgressions!
The close of our combat draws near;
A coupé, then a feint, then the finish!
(*He lunges.* VALVERT *staggers.* CYRANO *bows.*)
When I end the refrain, I draw blood.

(*Cheers. Applause from the boxes. Flowers and hand-kerchiefs are thrown down. Officers surround and congratulate* CYRANO. RAGUENEAU *dances with delight.* LE BRET *is both happy and appalled.* VALVERT's *friends lead him away, holding him up.*)

THE CROWD
(*In a long cry*)
Ah! . . .

A LIGHT-HORSEMAN
Magnificent!

A WOMAN
Charming!

RAGUENEAU
Phenomenal!

A MARQUIS
Unheard of!

LE BRET
Foolhardy!

THE CROWD
(*Swarming around* CYRANO)
Congratulations!—My compliments!—Bravo!

A WOMAN'S VOICE
He's a hero!

A MUSKETEER
(*Walking rapidly toward* CYRANO *with his hand out-stretched*)
Allow me to shake your hand, sir! It was a superb exploit, and I believe I can claim to be a judge of such things. It made me stamp my feet with joy!
(*Walks away.*)

CYRANO

(*To* CUIGY)
What is that gentleman's name?

CUIGY

D'Artagnan.*

LE BRET
(*To* CYRANO, *taking his arm*)
I'd like to have a talk with you.

CYRANO

Wait till this crowd thins out a little. (*To* BELLEROSE) May
I stay?

BELLEROSE

(*Respectfully*)
Of course, sir!
(*Shouts are heard from outside.*)

JODELET

(*Who has gone to look*)
Montfleury is being booed!

BELLEROSE

(*Solemnly*)
Sic transit! . . . (*Changing his tone, to the* DOORKEEPER
and the man who is preparing to put out the candles)
Sweep out the theater and lock the door, but leave the
candles burning. We'll come back after dinner to rehearse
the new farce we're going to present tomorrow.
(JODELET *and* BELLEROSE *go out, after bowing deeply to*
CYRANO.)

THE DOORKEEPER

(*To* CYRANO)
Aren't you going to dine, sir?

CYRANO

No.
(*The* DOORKEEPER *withdraws.*)

LE BRET

(*To* CYRANO)
Why not?

* Charles de Baatz, Seigneur d'Artagnan (1611–1673), an officer
who had an outstanding military career. The fictional hero of Alexandre Dumas' *The Three Musketeers* bears d'Artagnan's name and
is modeled on him to a certain extent.

CYRANO
(*Proudly*)
Because . . . (*Changing his tone, seeing that the* DOOR-
KEEPER *is out of earshot*) Because I have no money.

LE BRET
(*Making the gesture of throwing a bag*)
What! That bag of money . . .

CYRANO
Alas, my month's allotment lived only for a day!

LE BRET
And for the rest of the month . . .

CYRANO
I have nothing left.

LE BRET
What foolishness to throw it all away!

CYRANO
Yes, but what a gesture!

THE REFRESHMENT GIRL
(*Coughing from behind her little counter*)
Ahem! . . . (CYRANO *and* LE BRET *turn around. She comes
forward timidly.*) Sir, I . . . I can't bear to think of you
going hungry. (*Points to the refreshment table.*) I have
plenty of food here. . . . (*Wholeheartedly*) Take whatever
you like!

CYRANO
(*Gallantly taking off his hat*)
My dear child, my Gascon pride forbids me to accept the
slightest morsel from your fingers, but since I fear a refusal
would offend you, I will accept . . . (*Goes to the refreshment table and chooses.*) Oh, very little! One of these
grapes . . . (*She tries to give him the whole cluster; he
picks off a single grape.*) Only one! . . . This glass of water
. . . (*She tries to pour him a glass of wine; he stops her.*)
And half a macaroon. (*Breaks one and gives her back the
other half.*)

LE BRET
But that's ridiculous!

THE REFRESHMENT GIRL
Oh, please take something else!

CYRANO

I will. Your lovely hand.
(*She holds out her hand to him and he kisses it as if she were a princess.*)

THE REFRESHMENT GIRL

Thank you, sir. (*Bows.*) Good-by. (*Leaves.*)

Scene V

Cyrano, Le Bret, then the Doorkeeper.

CYRANO

(*To* LE BRET)
You wanted to have a talk with me? I'm ready to listen.
(*Sets the macaroon down on the refreshment table in front of him.*) My dinner! . . . (*Sets down the glass of water.*) My drink! . . . (*And finally the grape*) My dessert! (*Sits down.*) There, I'm ready to begin. I have an excellent appetite this evening. (*Eating*) What was it you wanted to tell me?

LE BRET

That you're going to have some badly distorted ideas if you listen only to those fools who like to give themselves such warlike airs. Talk with a few sensible people and you'll be better informed of the effect produced by your act of bravado.

CYRANO

(*Finishing his macaroon*)
It was enormous.

LE BRET

The Cardinal . . .

CYRANO

(*Beaming*)
The Cardinal was there?

LE BRET

Yes, and he must have found it . . .

CYRANO

Highly original, I'm sure.

LE BRET

But . . .

CYRANO

He's an author himself. He couldn't have been displeased to see another author's play disrupted.

LE BRET

You've made too many enemies!

CYRANO

About how many would you say I made today?

LE BRET

Forty-eight. Without counting the women.

CYRANO

(Beginning to eat his grape)
Really? That many?

LE BRET

Yes. First, there's Montfleury, then the burgher you kicked, De Guiche, Valvert, of course, Baro, the Academy . . .

CYRANO

Stop! That's already enough to delight me!

LE BRET

I don't understand the way you live. Where will it lead you? What are you trying to accomplish?

CYRANO

I was once confused and bewildered by all the complicated courses of action that were open to me. Finally I chose . . .

LE BRET

What did you choose?

CYRANO

The simplest course of all. I decided to be admirable in everything!

LE BRET

(Shrugging)
If you say so. . . . But let me ask you something else. What's the real reason for your hatred of Montfluery? You can tell *me* the truth.

CYRANO

(Standing up)
That bloated old sot, with a belly so big he can't touch his own navel, still considers himself a terror with the ladies and gives them amorous looks with those froglike eyes of his while he's bumbling his lines on the stage. I've hated him since the day when I saw him look at . . . It was like watching a slimy slug crawling on a flower!

LE BRET

(*Astonished*)
What's this? Do I understand you rightly? Is it possible
that . . .

CYRANO

(*With a bitter laugh*)
That I'm in love? (*Changing to a grave tone*) Yes, it's true.

LE BRET
May I ask with whom? You've never told me . . .

CYRANO

With whom I'm in love? Come now, think a moment: this
nose of mine, which precedes me by a quarter of an hour
wherever I go, forbids me ever to dream of being loved by
even an ugly woman. You ask me whom I love? The
answer should be clear to you! Whom else would I love
but the most beautiful woman in the world?

LE BRET
The most beautiful . . .

CYRANO

Of course! The most beautiful of all women! The most
captivating, the most intelligent . . . (*Dejectedly*) . . . the
blondest. . . .

LE BRET
For God's sake, tell me: who is she?

CYRANO

She's a mortal danger without meaning to be one; she's exquisite without giving it a thought; she's a trap set by
nature, a rose in which love lies in ambush! Anyone who
has seen her smile has known perfection. She creates grace
without movement, and makes all divinity fit into her slightest gesture. And neither Venus in her shell, nor Diana
striding in the great, blossoming forest, can compare to
her when she goes through the streets of Paris in her sedan
chair!

LE BRET
Now I believe I know! It *is* becoming clear!

CYRANO
It's perfectly transparent.

LE BRET
Your cousin, Magdeleine Robin?

CYRANO

Yes—Roxane.

LE BRET

Then you ought to be overjoyed! You love her? Tell her so!
You've covered yourself with glory in her eyes today.

CYRANO

Look at me and tell me what hope this protuberance might
leave me! I have no illusions. Sometimes, in the blue
shadows of evening, I give way to tender feelings. I go into
a garden, smelling the fragrance of spring with my poor
monstrous nose, and watch a man and a woman strolling
together in the moonlight. I think how much I, too, would
like to be walking arm in arm with a woman, under the
moon. I let myself be carried away, I forget myself—
and then I suddenly see the shadow of my profile on the
garden wall.

LE BRET

(*Deeply moved*)
My friend . . .

CYRANO

My friend, I have bad moments now and then, feeling myself so ugly, all alone. . . .

LE BRET

(*With concern, taking his hand*)
Do you weep?

CYRANO

Oh, no, never! No, it would be grotesque if a tear ran down
this nose! As long as it's in my power to prevent it, I'll
never let the divine beauty of tears be sullied by such
gross ugliness. There's nothing more sublime than tears,
and I wouldn't want a single one of them to become an
object of ridicule because of me.

LE BRET

Come, don't be sad! Love is only a game of chance!

CYRANO

(*Shaking his head*)
No! I love Cleopatra—do I look like a Caesar? I adore
Berenice—have I the appearance of a Titus?

LE BRET

But you're overlooking your courage, your wit! . . . Take
that girl who offered to give you dinner just now, for ex-

ample: you could see for yourself that she was far from detesting you!

CYRANO
(*Struck by this realization*)
Yes, it's true!

LE BRET
Well, then? You see? And Roxane herself was pale as she watched your duel. . . .

CYRANO
Pale?

LE BRET
You've already made a deep impression on her heart and her mind. Don't be timid: speak to her, tell her, so that . . .

CYRANO
So that she'll laugh in my face? No! That's the one thing in the world that I fear!

THE DOORKEEPER
(*Bringing in Roxane's* DUENNA)
Sir, this lady would like to speak to you.

CYRANO
(*Seeing the* DUENNA)
My God! Her duenna!

Scene VI

Cyrano, Le Bret, the Duenna.

THE DUENNA
(*With a deep bow*)
My lady wishes me to ask her valiant cousin where she can see him in private.

CYRANO
(*Thunderstruck*)
See me?

THE DUENNA
(*With another bow*)
Yes. She has things to tell you.

CYRANO
Things to . . .

THE DUENNA

(*Bowing again*)
To tell you.

CYRANO

(*Unsteady on his feet*)
My God!

THE DUENNA

She will go to early Mass at the Saint-Roch church to-morrow morning.

CYRANO

(*Clutching* LE BRET *to steady himself*)
Ah, my God!

THE DUENNA

When she leaves the church, where can she go to talk with you?

CYRANO

(*Agitated*)
Where? . . . I . . . My God! . . . Where . . .

THE DUENNA

Well?

CYRANO

I'm trying to think!

THE DUENNA

Tell me.

CYRANO

At . . . at Ragueneau's shop . . . Ragueneau, the pastry cook. . . .

THE DUENNA

Where is it?

CYRANO

It's . . . it's on . . . Oh, my God! . . . It's on the . . . the Rue Saint-Honoré!

THE DUENNA

(*Withdrawing*)
Very well. At seven o'clock.

CYRANO

I'll be there.
(*The* DUENNA *leaves.*)

Scene VII

Cyrano, Le Bret, then the Actors and Actresses, Cuigy,
Brissaille, Lignière, the Doorkeeper, the Violinists.

CYRANO

(*Falling into* LE BRET'*s arms*)
Me! She wants to see *me!*

LE BRET

I see your sadness has vanished!

CYRANO

Ah, for whatever reason, she knows I exist!

LE BRET

Please be calm.

CYRANO

No! I'm going to be frenzied and turbulent! I need a whole
army to vanquish! I have ten hearts, twenty arms! It's no
longer enough for me to cut down dwarfs . . . (*Shouts at
the top of his lungs.*) . . . I need giants!
(*For some time now, the* ACTORS *and* ACTRESSES *have
been moving on the stage: the rehearsal is beginning. The*
VIOLINISTS *have taken their places.*)

A VOICE

(*From the stage*)
Quiet! We're rehearsing!

CYRANO

(*Laughing*)
And we're leaving!
(*He goes upstage. Through the entrance of the theater
come* CUIGY, BRISSAILLE, *and several* OFFICERS *holding
up* LIGNIÈRE, *who is thoroughly drunk.*)

CUIGY

Cyrano!

CYRANO

What is it?

CUIGY

We've brought a friend—much the worse for wine!

CYRANO

(*Recognizing him*)
Lignière! . . . What's happened to you?

CUIGY

He wants to see you.

BRISSAILLE

He can't go home.

CYRANO

Why not?

LIGNIÈRE

(*In a thick voice, holding up a rumpled piece of paper*)
This note warns me . . . hundred men against me . . . because of . . . of a song . . . great danger . . . Porte de
Nesle . . . on my way home. . . . Will you let me . . . let
me sleep under your roof tonight?

CYRANO

A hundred men, you say? You'll sleep at home tonight!

LIGNIÈRE

(*Alarmed*)
But . . .

CYRANO

(*In a thunderous voice, pointing to the lighted lantern
that the* DOORKEEPER *has been holding while curiously
listening to this scene*)
Take that lantern . . . (LIGNIÈRE *quickly obeys.*) . . . and
walk! I'll cover you! (*To the* OFFICERS) And you, follow at
a distance: you'll be witnesses!

CUIGY

But a hundred men! . . .

CYRANO

I need at least that many this evening!
(*The* ACTORS *and* ACTRESSES, *in their various costumes,
have come down from the stage and approached the
group.*)

LE BRET

But why should you risk your life . . .

CYRANO

Le Bret is grumbling again!

LE BRET

. . . for this drunkard?

CYRANO

(*Patting* LIGNIÈRE's *shoulder*)
Because this drunkard, this walking wine cask, once did
something admirable. When he saw the woman he loved

taking holy water as she was leaving church after Mass, he hurried to the font, and even though he ordinarily can't bear even the sight of water, drank it all!

AN ACTRESS

(*Wearing a soubrette costume*)
That was a lovely thing to do!

CYRANO

Yes, wasn't it?

THE ACTRESS

(*To the others*)
But why should there be a hundred men against one poor poet?

CYRANO

Let's go! (*To the* OFFICERS) Gentlemen, when you see me charge, don't come to my assistance, no matter how great the danger!

ANOTHER ACTRESS

(*Leaping down from the stage*)
I want to go and watch!

CYRANO

Come along!

A THIRD ACTRESS

(*Also leaping down from the stage, to an old* ACTOR)
Are you coming, Cassandre?

CYRANO

Yes, come, all of you: the Doctor, Isabelle, Léandre—everyone! You'll form a gay, charming troupe that will add a note of Italian farce to this Spanish drama, and you'll surround its solemnity with the merry sound of your chatter, like jingling bells around a tambourine!

ALL THE WOMEN

(*Jumping for joy*)
Bravo!—Quick, a cloak!—Where's my hood?

JODELET

We're off!

CYRANO

(*To the* VIOLINISTS)
You, gentlemen, will inspire us with your music as we march. (*The* VIOLINISTS *join the procession that is forming. Lighted candles are taken from the footlights and distributed. The scene takes on the aspect of a torchlight parade.*)

Bravo! Officers, ladies in costume, and twenty paces in front . . . (*He takes up the station he has described.*) . . . I will walk alone, under the plume that glory herself has placed on my hat, with twice the pride of Scipio, and a nose three times as long! . . . Remember, now: no one is allowed to lift a finger to help me! . . . All ready? One, two, three! Doorkeeper, open the door! (*The* DOORKEEPER *opens both halves of the door, giving a glimpse of picturesque old Paris in the moonlight.*) Ah, Paris lies before us, dim and nebulous in the shadows, with moonlight flowing down the slopes of her roofs! An exquisite setting for the scene about to be performed! There, beneath the mist, the Seine quivers like a mysterious magic mirror. . . . And you will see what you will see!

ALL

To the Porte de Nesle!

CYRANO

(*Standing on the threshold*)
To the Porte de Nesle! (*Turns to the* SOUBRETTE.) You asked, mademoiselle, why a hundred men had been sent to attack one poet. (*Calmly, drawing his sword*) I'll tell you: it's because that poet is known to be a friend of mine. (*He goes out. The procession*—LIGNIÈRE *staggering in the lead, then the* ACTRESSES *on the arms of the* OFFICERS, *then the* ACTORS, *gamboling lightheartedly*—*moves forward into the night, to the sound of the violins, and in the dim glow of the candles.*)

CURTAIN

ACT TWO

The Poets' Cookshop

The large workroom of the shop of Ragueneau, cookshop proprietor and pastry cook, at the corner of the Rue Saint-Honoré and the Rue de l'Arbre-Sec. The street, seen through the panes of the door in the background, is gray in the first glow of dawn.

Downstage left, a counter surrounded by a wrought-iron canopy from which geese, ducks, and white peacocks are hanging. Large china vases hold tall bouquets of common flowers, mainly sunflowers. On the same side, further back, an immense fireplace in front of which, between the monstrous andirons, each one supporting a small pot, roasts are dripping into grease pans.

Downstage right, a door. Behind it, a staircase leading up to a small room with a sloping ceiling, seen through open shutters. A table has been set here, and a small Flemish chandelier lighted; it is a room for eating and drinking. A wooden gallery, extending from the top of the stairs, seems to lead to other such rooms.

In the middle of the workroom, various kinds of game are hung from an iron hoop that can be lowered by a rope, forming a culinary chandelier. The red glow of the ovens can be seen in the shadows under the staircase. Copper pots and pans are gleaming. Spits are

58

turning. Pyramids of elaborate pastry, hams hanging from the ceiling.

The morning rush has begun. Fat cooks, distraught scullions, and small kitchen boys are jostling one another in a profusion of hats adorned with chicken feathers or guinea-fowl wings. Mounds of brioches and vast arrays of petits fours are being carried on wicker trays and sheets of metal.

Some tables are covered with cakes and dishes. Others, surrounded by chairs, are awaiting eaters and drinkers. A smaller one in a corner is laden with papers. Ragueneau is seated at it, writing, as the curtain rises.

Scene I

Ragueneau, Pastrycooks, then Lise; Ragueneau at the little table, writing with an inspired air and counting on his fingers.

FIRST PASTRYCOOK
(Bringing a complicated construction on a tray)
Fruit in nougat!

SECOND PASTRYCOOK
(Bringing a dish)
Custard!

THIRD PASTRYCOOK
(Bringing a roast decorated with feathers)
Peacock!

FOURTH PASTRYCOOK
(Bringing a sheet of metal)
Cakes!

FIFTH PASTRYCOOK
(Bringing an earthenware pot)
Braised beef!
(RAGUENEAU stops writing and looks up.)

RAGUENEAU
The silver of dawn is already gleaming on the copper pots! Silence the god who sings within you, Ragueneau! The hour of the lute will come—it is now the hour of the oven! *(Stands up and speaks to a COOK.)* There's something lacking in this sauce.

THE COOK

What shall I do to it?

RAGUENEAU

Make it a little more lyrical.

THE COOK

(Puzzled)
What?

FIRST PASTRYCOOK

Tarts!

SECOND PASTRYCOOK

Pies!

RAGUENEAU
(In front of the fireplace)
Away, my Muse, lest your eyes be reddened by this mundane fire! *(To a* PASTRYCOOK, *pointing to some round loaves of bread)* The slit in these loaves is badly placed: the caesura should be in the middle, between the hemistitches! *(To another, pointing to an unfinished pie)* This palace of crust must have a roof. *(To a young* APPRENTICE *who is sitting on the floor, placing poultry on a spit)* Alternate the humble chickens with the stately turkeys on your spit, my son, as Malherbe* alternated long and short lines in his verse, and then turn stanzas of poultry above the fire!

ANOTHER APPRENTICE
(Bringing a tray covered with a cloth)
I've baked this in your honor, sir. I hope it will please you.
(He uncovers the tray, revealing a large pastry lyre.)

RAGUENEAU

(Enraptured)
A lyre!

THE APPRENTICE

Made of pastry dough.

RAGUENEAU

(Deeply moved)
With candied fruit!

THE APPRENTICE

And I made the strings of sugar.

* François de Malherbe (1555–1628), a French poet who laid down precise and rigid rules for poetry.

RAGUENEAU

(Giving him some money)
Here, go and drink to my health! *(Sees* LISE *coming in.)*
My wife! Quickly, go about your business—and hide that
money! *(To* LISE, *pointing to the lyre with embarrassment)*
Isn't it beautiful?

LISE

It's ridiculous!
   (She puts a pile of paper bags on the counter.)

RAGUENEAU

You've brought some paper bags? Good, thank you. *(Looks
at them more closely.)* Oh, no! My treasured books! My
friends' poetry! Desecrated, dismembered, to make bags for
pastry! You're as heartless as the Bacchantes who tore Or-
pheus to pieces!

LISE

(Sharply)
I have a right to make use of what your wretched scribblers
leave here as their only payment!

RAGUENEAU

Don't insult those divine songbirds, you vulture!

LISE

You never called me such names before that rabble began
coming here!

RAGUENEAU

(Pointing to the bags)
How can you treat poetry with such disrespect?

LISE

I'll treat poetry however I please!

RAGUENEAU

I shudder to think of what you might do with prose!

Scene II

The same, with two Children who have just entered.

RAGUENEAU

What will you have, children?

FIRST CHILD

Three small pies, please.

RAGUENEAU

(*Serving them*)
Three small pies, hot and brown!

SECOND CHILD
Would you please wrap them?

RAGUENEAU

(*Aside, with dismay*)
Alas! One of my bags. . . . (*To the* CHILDREN) Very well.
(*Picks up a bag, and as he is about to put the pies into it,
reads from it.*) "Like Ulysses parting from Penelope . . ."
No, not this one! (*Sets the bag aside and takes another.
Reads.*) "Phoebus of the golden hair . . ." Not this one!
(*Puts it down.*)

LISE

(*Impatiently*)
Well, what are you waiting for?

RAGUENEAU
Nothing, nothing. . . . (*Takes a third bag and resigns himself to using it.*) The sonnet to Phyllis! What a loss!

LISE

(*Shrugging*)
I'm glad you finally made up your mind, you poor simple-
ton!

(*She stands on a chair and begins putting dishes away on
a shelf. As soon as her back is turned,* RAGUENEAU *calls
back the* CHILDREN, *who are already at the door.*)

RAGUENEAU

Psst! . . . Children! . . . Give me back the sonnet to Phyllis
and I'll give you six pies instead of three! (*The* CHILDREN
*give him the bag, quickly take the pies, and leave. He
smooths the rumpled bag and begins reading.*) "Phyllis . . ."
A spot of butter on that lovely name! "Phyllis . . ."
(CYRANO *enters abruptly.*)

Scene III

Ragueneau, Lise, Cyrano, then the Musketeer.

CYRANO
What time is it?

RAGUENEAU
(*Bowing to him*)
Six o'clock.

CYRANO
(*With great emotion*)
One more hour!
(*He begins pacing the floor.*)

RAGUENEAU
(*Following him*)
Congratulations!

CYRANO
For what?

RAGUENEAU
I saw your duel!

CYRANO
Which one?

RAGUENEAU
At the Hôtel de Bourgogne!

CYRANO
(*Disdainfully*)
Oh, that one. . . .

RAGUENEAU
(*Admiringly*)
A duel in verse!

LISE
He talks about nothing else!

CYRANO
I'm glad to hear it.

RAGUENEAU
(*Lunging with a spit that he has picked up*)
"When I end the refrain, I draw blood! . . . When I end
the refrain, I draw blood!" Magnificent! (*With growing enthusiasm*) "When I end the refrain . . ."

CYRANO
What time is it, Ragueneau?

RAGUENEAU
(*Looking at the clock while holding the position of the
lunge he has just made*)
Five past six. ". . . I draw blood!" (*Stands up straight.*) Ah,
what a ballade!

LISE
(*To* CYRANO, *who has absentmindedly shaken her hand while passing by her counter*)
Your hand is wounded!

CYRANO
It's nothing, just a small gash.

RAGUENEAU
Have you been doing something dangerous?

CYRANO
No, I've been in no danger.

LISE
(*Shaking her finger at him*)
I believe you're telling a lie!

CYRANO
Why? Was my nose twitching? If so, it must have been an enormous lie! (*Changing his tone*) I'm waiting for someone here. If I don't wait in vain, I want you to leave us alone together.

RAGUENEAU
I can't do that: my poets will soon be here.

LISE
(*Sarcastically*)
For their first meal!

CYRANO
You will take them away when I give you a signal. . . . What time is it?

RAGUENEAU
Ten past six.

CYRANO
(*Nervously sitting down at* RAGUENEAU's *table and taking a sheet of paper*)
May I have a pen?

RAGUENEAU
(*Giving him the pen he has been carrying behind his ear*)
Here, take my swan's feather!
(*A* MUSKETEER *with a superb mustache enters.*)

THE MUSKETEER
(*In a stentorian voice*)
Greetings!
(LISE *hurries toward him.*)

CYRANO
(*Looking around*)
Who's that?

RAGUENEAU
A friend of my wife's. A mighty warrior—according to what he says! He ...

CYRANO
(*Taking his pen again and waving* RAGUENEAU *away*)
Never mind. (*To himself*) Write a note ... fold it ... give it to her ... run away. .... (*Throws down the pen.*) Coward! You don't have the courage to say one word to her! (*To* RAGUENEAU) What time is it?

RAGUENEAU
Quarter past six.

CYRANO
(*To himself*)
I'm afraid to speak a single one of all the words I have in here. (*Strikes his chest.*) But writing is a different matter. ... (*Takes his pen again.*) I'll now put down on paper the love letter that I've already written within myself a hundred times. I have only to look into my soul and copy the words inscribed in it.
(*He begins writing. Through the glass of the door, thin figures are seen moving hesitantly.*)

Scene IV

Ragueneau, Lise, the Musketeer, Cyrano, writing at the little table, the Poets, dressed in black, with sagging, muddy stockings.

LISE
(*Entering, to* RAGUENEAU)
Here come your mud-spattered poets!

FIRST POET
(*Entering, to* RAGUENEAU)
Colleague!

SECOND POET
(*Taking* RAGUENEAU's *hand*)
Dear colleague!

THIRD POET

Eagle of pastry cooks! (*Sniffs.*) What a fragrant nest you have!

FOURTH POET

O culinary god!

FIFTH POET

Apollo of the kitchen!

RAGUENEAU
(*Surrounded, embraced, shaken*)
They always make me feel at ease as soon as they come in!

FIRST POET

We were delayed by a crowd gathered at the Porte de Nesle.

SECOND POET

Eight bandits had been felled by swordplay and lay bleeding on the pavement!

CYRANO
(*Briefly looking up*)
Eight? I thought there were only seven.
(*Resumes writing his letter.*)

RAGUENEAU
(*To* CYRANO)
Do you know the hero of that combat?

CYRANO
(*Casually*)
No.

LISE
(*To the* MUSKETEER)
And you?

THE MUSKETEER
(*Twirling his mustache*)
Perhaps!

CYRANO
(*Writing*)
"I love you. . . ."
(*He is heard murmuring from time to time.*)

FIRST POET

We were told that one man had routed a whole band of assassins!

SECOND POET

There were pikes and clubs strewn all over the ground!

CYRANO

(*Writing*)
"Your eyes . . ."

THIRD POET

And hats were found as far away as the Quai des Orfèvres!

FIRST POET

The man who could do a thing like that . . .

CYRANO

(*Writing*)
"Your lips . . ."

FIRST POET

. . . must have been some sort of ferocious giant!

CYRANO

(*Writing*)
". . . and I become faint with fear each time I see you."

SECOND POET

(*Snatching a cake*)
What have you been writing, Ragueneau?

CYRANO

(*Writing*)
"Your faithful worshiper . . ." (*He stops as he is about to sign his name, stands up, and puts the letter in his doublet.*) No need to sign it, since I'll give it to her myself.

RAGUENEAU

(*To the* SECOND POET)
I've written a recipe in verse.

THIRD POET

(*Sitting down next to a tray of cream puffs*)
Let's hear it!

FOURTH POET

(*Looking at a brioche that he has picked up*)
This brioche has put its hat on crooked.
(*Bites off the top of it.*)

FIRST POET

This gingerbread gazes at a hungry poet with its almond eyes and warm, inviting smile!
(*Takes the piece of gingerbread.*)

SECOND POET

(*To* RAGUENEAU)
We're listening.

THIRD POET
(Lightly squeezing a cream puff between his fingers)
See how this cream puff drools with delight!

SECOND POET
(Biting into the pastry lyre)
For the first time, the Lyre gives me sustenance!

RAGUENEAU
(Clears his throat, straightens his hat, strikes a pose, and prepares to recite.)
A recipe in verse . . .

SECOND POET
(To the first, nudging him)
Are you having breakfast?

FIRST POET
(To the second)
Yes, and you're eating dinner!

RAGUENEAU
"How to Make Almond Tarts"

Beat some eggs till they are foamy;
Mix with tangy citron juice;
Then fold in sweet milk of almonds.
Line your pans with pastry dough,
Slowly pour your foam to fill them;
Let them bake till golden brown.
Now remove them from the oven:
Luscious, dainty almond tarts!

THE POETS
(With their mouths full)
Exquisite! Delightful!

A POET
(Choking)
Omph!
(They go upstage, still eating. CYRANO, who has been watching, approaches RAGUENEAU.)

CYRANO
Haven't you ever noticed how they stuff themselves while they listen to your verse?

RAGUENEAU
(In a low voice, with a smile)
Of course, but I never let them know it, because I don't want to embarrass them. I take double pleasure in reciting

my compositions like that: I satisfy my little weakness, and at the same time I feed brother poets who would otherwise go hungry.

CYRANO
(*Affectionately clapping him on the shoulder*)
You're a fine fellow, Ragueneau! (RAGUENEAU *goes to rejoin his friends.* CYRANO *watches him walk away, then speaks rather brusquely.*) Lise! (LISE, *in tender conversation with the* MUSKETEER, *starts, and then comes toward* CYRANO.) Is that musketeer laying siege to you?

LISE
(*Offended*)
If a man tries to attack my virtue, I stop him with a single withering look.

CYRANO
"Withering" is hardly the word to describe the look you were giving your friend just now.

LISE
(*Taken aback*)
But . . .

CYRANO
(*Bluntly*)
I like Ragueneau. That's why I won't allow anyone to make him play the ridiculous part of a deceived husband.

LISE
But . . .

CYRANO
(*Raising his voice in order to be heard by the* MUSKETEER)
A word to the wise. . . .
(*He bows to the* MUSKETEER *and goes to take up his observation post at the door in the background, after looking at the clock.*)

LISE
(*To the* MUSKETEER, *who has merely returned* CYRANO's *bow in silence*)
Well? Aren't you going to say anything? I'm surprised you haven't already thrown your answer against his nose!

THE MUSKETEER
His nose? Oh, his nose! . . .
(*He quickly walks away.* LISE *follows him.*)

CYRANO

(*From the door in the background,* motioning RAGUEN-
EAU *to take the* POETS *away*)
Psst! . . .

RAGUENEAU

(*Showing the* POETS *the door on the right*)
Come this way, gentlemen, we'll be much more comfort-
able . . .

CYRANO

(*Impatiently*)
Psst! psst!

RAGUENEAU

(*Leading them away*)
. . . for reading poetry.

FIRST POET

(*Despairingly, with his mouth full*)
But what about the cakes?

SECOND POET

Let's take them with us!
(*They all go out behind* RAGUENEAU, *in procession, after
having snatched up several trays of pastry.*)

Scene V

Cyrano, Roxane, the Duenna.

CYRANO

I'll give her my letter if I feel that there's the slightest hope!
(ROXANE, *masked, appears behind the glass of the door,
followed by the* DUENNA. *He throws open the door.*) Come
in! (*Takes the* DUENNA *aside.*) May I have a word with
you?

THE DUENNA

Have several, if you like.

CYRANO

Are you fond of pastry?

THE DUENNA

I'm sinfully fond of it!

CYRANO

(*Quickly taking some of the paper bags on the counter*)
Good. Here are two sonnets by Monsieur Benserade . . .

THE DUENNA

(*Disappointed*)
Oh. . . .

CYRANO

. . . which I will fill with custard tarts for you.
(*The* DUENNA's *face brightens.*)

THE DUENNA

Ah!

CYRANO

Do you like cream puffs?

THE DUENNA

(*With dignity*)
I hold them in high regard.

CYRANO

Here are six of them for you, in a poem by Saint-Amant.
And in this verse by Chapelain* I'll place a piece of butter
cake. You really like pastry, do you?

THE DUENNA

I adore it!

CYRANO

(*Loading her arms with filled bags*)
Then I'm sure you'll enjoy going out and eating all this in
the street.

THE DUENNA

But . . .

CYRANO

(*Pushing her outside*)
And please don't come back until you've finished.
(*He closes the door, approaches* ROXANE, *and stops at
a respectful distance with his hat in his hand.*)

Scene VI

Cyrano, Roxane, the Duenna for a moment.

CYRANO

May this day be blessed above all others: the day when

* Marc-Antoine de Gérard, Sieur de Saint-Amant (1594–1661), and
Jean Chapelain (1595–1674): poets who were among the original
members of the French Academy.

you ceased to forget my existence and came here to tell
me . . . to tell me? . . .

ROXANE

(*Who has taken off her mask*)
First let me thank you for humbling that arrogant fop with
your sword yesterday, because he's the man whom a certain great lord, infatuated with me . . .

CYRANO

De Guiche?

ROXANE

(*Lowering her eyes*)
. . . was trying to impose on me as . . . as a husband. . . .

CYRANO

A husband only for the sake of form? (*Bows.*) I'm happy
to know that I fought not for my ugly nose, but for your
beautiful eyes.

ROXANE

And then, I wanted to tell you . . . But before I make my
confession, give me time to see you again as I did in the
past, when I thought of you almost as my brother. We used
to play together in the park, beside the lake. . . .

CYRANO

Yes. . . . You came to Bergerac every summer.

ROXANE

You used a reed for a sword in those days!

CYRANO

And you used corn silk to make hair for your dolls.

ROXANE

We played all sorts of games.

CYRANO

And ate blackberries before they were ripe.

ROXANE

You always did whatever I wanted!

CYRANO

You weren't yet known as Roxane. In short skirts, you
were still called Magdeleine.

ROXANE

Was I pretty then?

CYRANO

You weren't ugly.

ROXANE

Sometimes you came to me with your hand bleeding from some accident and I acted as if I were your mother, trying to make my voice stern. (*Takes his hand.*) "What's this?" I'd say. "Have you hurt yourself again?" (*Looks at his hand.*) Oh! Even now! You've done it again! (CYRANO *tries to withdraw his hand.*) No! Let me see! You're still hurting yourself, at your age! How did you do it this time?

CYRANO

I was playing again—at the Porte de Nesle.

ROXANE

(*Sits down at a table and wets her handkerchief in a glass of water.*)
Give me that hand!

CYRANO

(*Also sits down.*)
You still mother me!

ROXANE

While I wash away this blood, I want you to describe what happened. How many were there against you?

CYRANO

Oh, not quite a hundred.

ROXANE

Tell me about it!

CYRANO

No, never mind. Tell me what you couldn't bring yourself to say just now.

ROXANE

(*Without letting go of his hand*)
Yes, I can say it now that the past has returned to encourage me. Here it is. I'm in love with someone.

CYRANO

Ah! ...

ROXANE

Someone who doesn't know.

CYRANO

Ah! ...

ROXANE

Not yet.

CYRANO

Ah! ...

ROXANE

But he *will* know soon.

CYRANO

Ah! ...

ROXANE

He's a poor man who till now has loved me timidly, from a distance, without daring to say anything.

CYRANO

Ah! ...

ROXANE

Let me keep your hand, it feels feverish. . . . But I've seen a confession of love trembling on his lips.

CYRANO

Ah! ...

ROXANE
(Bandaging his hand with her handkerchief)
And it so happens, cousin, that he's a member of your regiment.

CYRANO

Ah! ...

ROXANE

(Smiling)
In fact, he's a Cadet in your company!

CYRANO

Ah! ...

ROXANE

His face shines with wit and intelligence. He's proud, noble, young, fearless, handsome. . . .

CYRANO
(Standing up, with a stricken expression)
Handsome!

ROXANE

What is it? What's the matter?

CYRANO

Nothing. . . . It's . . . it's . . . (*Shows her his hand, with a smile.*) It's only a twinge of pain from this little scratch.

ROXANE

Well, I love him, even though I've never seen him anywhere but in the theater.

CYRANO

You've never spoken to each other?

ROXANE

Only with our eyes.

CYRANO

Then how do you know he loves you?

ROXANE

Under the linden trees of the Place Royale, people gossip.
... Talkative acquaintances have told me. ...

CYRANO

You say he's a Cadet?

ROXANE

Yes, in the Guards.

CYRANO

His name?

ROXANE

Baron Christian de Neuvillette.

CYRANO

Neuvillette? There's no Cadet by that name.

ROXANE

There is now. He began serving only this morning, under
Captain Carbon de Castel-Jaloux.

CYRANO

You've lost your heart so quickly! But, my poor girl . . .

THE DUENNA
(*Opening the door in the background*)
I've eaten all the pastry, Monsieur de Bergerac!

CYRANO

Then read the poetry on the bags! (*The* DUENNA *disappears.*) My poor girl, you're so fond of fine words and
gracious wit—what if he should prove to be an uncultured
savage?

ROXANE

Impossible. He has the hair of one of d'Urfé's* heroes!

* Honoré d'Urfé (1567–1625), French novelist whose heroes were
taken as paragons of chivalrous manhood in the seventeenth century.

CYRANO
His speech may be as crude as his hair is elegant.

ROXANE
No, there's delicacy in everything he says. I feel it!

CYRANO
Yes, all words are delicate when they come from lips adorned with a shapely mustache. . . . But what if he's a fool?

ROXANE
(Stamping her foot)
Then I'll die! There, are you satisfied?

CYRANO
(After a time)
You brought me here to tell me this? I confess I don't quite understand why.

ROXANE
It's because someone terrified me yesterday by telling me that most of you in your company are Gascons, and . . .

CYRANO
And that we always provoke a duel with any newcomer who gains the favor of being admitted among us without being a Gascon? Is that what you were told?

ROXANE
Yes. You can imagine how I trembled for him when I heard it!

CYRANO
(Aside)
And with good reason!

ROXANE
But when I saw you yesterday, great and invincible, punishing that scoundrel and holding all those brutes at bay, I said to myself, "Everyone fears him. If he were willing to . . ."

CYRANO
Very well, I'll protect your little baron.

ROXANE
Oh, I knew you would! I've always had such tender affection for you. . . .

CYRANO
Yes, yes.

ROXANE

You'll be his friend?

CYRANO

I will.

ROXANE

And he'll never have a duel?

CYRANO

No. I promise.

ROXANE

I knew I was right to like you so much! And now I must go. (*Quickly puts on her mask and speaks distractedly.*) But you haven't told me about your battle last night. It must have been incredible! . . . Tell him to write to me. (*Throws him a kiss.*) Oh, I love you!

CYRANO

Yes, yes.

ROXANE

A hundred men against you? Well, good-by. You're my best friend!

CYRANO

Yes, yes.

ROXANE

Tell him to write! . . . A hundred men! You'll tell me about it some other time; I can't stay now. A hundred men! What courage!

CYRANO

(*Bowing to her*)
Oh, I've done better since then.
(*She leaves. He remains motionless, looking down at the floor. A silence, then the door opens and* RAGUENEAU *puts in his head.*)

Scene VII

Cyrano, Ragueneau, the Poets, Carbon de Castel-Jaloux, the Cadets, the Crowd, etc., then De Guiche.

RAGUENEAU

May we come back in?

CYRANO

(Without moving)
Yes.
(RAGUENEAU *signals to his friends and they come in. At
the same time* CARBON DE CASTEL-JALOUX, *dressed as a
Captain of the Guards, appears at the door in the back-
ground and makes broad gestures when he sees* CYRANO.)

CARBON

Here he is!

CYRANO

(Looking up)
Captain!

CARBON

(Exultant)
Our hero! We know all about it! Thirty of my Cadets are
here!

CYRANO

(Stepping back)
But . . .

CARBON

(Trying to lead him out)
Come! They want to see you!

CYRANO

No!

CARBON

They're drinking in the tavern across the street, the Croix
du Trahoir.

CYRANO

I . . .

CARBON

*(Goes back to the doorway and shouts through it in a
thunderous voice.)*
Our hero won't come! He's in a bad mood!

A VOICE

(From outside)
Sandious!*
(Tumult outside, with a clatter of swords approaching)

* A Gascon exclamation, as are *mille dioux, capdedious, mordious,*
and *pocapdedious,* below.

CARBON
(*Rubbing his hands together*)
Here they come!

THE CADETS
(*Entering*)
Mille dioux!—Capdedious!—Mordious!—Pocapdedious!

RAGUENEAU
(*Stepping back in alarm*)
Gentlemen, your language tells me that you're all from Gascony!

THE CADETS
Yes, all of us!

A CADET
(*To* CYRANO)
Bravo!

CYRANO
(*Nodding*)
Baron.

SECOND CADET
(*Shaking* CYRANO's *hands*)
Hurrah!

CYRANO
Baron.

THIRD CADET
Let me embrace you!

CYRANO
Baron.

SEVERAL CADETS
Let's all embrace him!

CYRANO
(*Not knowing which one to answer*)
Baron ... Baron ... please. ...

RAGUENEAU
Are you all barons, gentlemen?

THE CADETS
All?

RAGUENEAU
Yes.

FIRST CADET

We could build a tower with our baronial coronets!

LE BRET
(*Entering and hurrying to* CYRANO)
Everyone wants to see you! There's a wild crowd led by those who were with you last night. . . .

CYRANO
(*Alarmed*)
You didn't tell them I was here, did you?

LE BRET
(*Rubbing his hands together*)
Of course I did!

A BURGHER
(*Entering, followed by a group*)
Sir, all the fashionable people in Paris are coming here!
(*Outside, the street is filled with people. Sedan chairs and carriages are stopping.*)

LE BRET
(*Softly, smiling at* CYRANO)
Have you seen Roxane?

CYRANO
(*Sharply*)
Quiet!

THE CROWD
(*Shouting from outside*)
Cyrano!
(*A throng bursts into the shop. Jostling. Cheers.*)

RAGUENEAU
(*Standing on a table*)
They're invading my shop! They're breaking everything! It's magnificent!

PEOPLE
(*Around* CYRANO)
My friend!—My friend!

CYRANO
I didn't have so many friends yesterday!

LE BRET
(*Delighted*)
What a triumph!

A YOUNG MARQUIS
(*Rushing toward* CYRANO *with hands outstretched*)
If you only knew, my dear Cyrano . . .

CYRANO
Your dear Cyrano? How can I have endeared myself to you when I've never seen you before?

ANOTHER MARQUIS
Sir, I'd like to introduce you to some ladies who are outside in my carriage.

CYRANO
(*Coldly*)
And who will introduce me to *you?*

LE BRET
(*Surprised*)
What's the matter with you?

CYRANO
Quiet!

A MAN OF LETTERS
(*With a writing case*)
Would you give me a few details of . . .

CYRANO
No.

LE BRET
(*Nudging him*)
That's Théophraste Renaudot!*

CYRANO
Well, what of it?

LE BRET
He's the inventor of the gazette, that printed sheet which tells so many things. They say it's an idea with a great future.

A POET
(*Coming forward*)
Sir . . .

CYRANO
Another one!

* Théophraste Renaudot (1586–1653) founded the first French newspaper in 1631, originally titled *La Gazette,* then *La Gazette de France.* In seventeenth-century France, "gazette" was the generic word for "newspaper."

THE POET

I want to compose a pentacrostic on your name. . . .

A MAN

(*Also coming forward*)

Sir . . .

CYRANO

Enough!

(*Movement, then the disorder of the crowd begins to subside.* DE GUICHE *enters, escorted by* OFFICERS, *then* CUIGY, BRISSAILLE, *and the* OFFICERS *who left with* CYRANO *at the end of Act I.* CUIGY *hurries to* CYRANO.)

CUIGY

(*To* CYRANO)

Monsieur de Guiche . . . (*Murmurs. Everyone stands aside.*) . . . has come with a message from Marshal de Gassion!

DE GUICHE

(*Bowing to* CYRANO)

The Marshal has just learned of your latest exploit and wishes me to express his admiration to you.

THE CROWD

Bravo!

CYRANO

(*Bowing*)

The Marhsal is an authority on daring deeds.

DE GUICHE

He would never have believed it if these gentlemen hadn't sworn to have seen it.

CUIGY

With our own eyes!

LE BRET

(*Aside, to* CYRANO, *who appears to be distracted*)

Aren't you going to . . .

CYRANO

Quiet!

LE BRET

You seem to be suffering!

CYRANO

(*Starting, then quickly drawing himself erect*)

In front of all these people? (*His mustache bristles; he throws out his chest.*) I, suffering? You'll see!

DE GUICHE

(*To whom* CUIGY *has been whispering*)
Your career is already rich in noble exploits. You serve
with those wild Gascons, don't you?

CYRANO

Yes, I'm a Cadet in the Guards.

A CADET

(*With fierce pride*)
He's one of us!

DE GUICHE

(*Looking at the Gascons grouped behind* CYRANO)
Ah! Then all these haughty-looking gentlemen are the
famous . . .

CARBON

Cyrano!

CYRANO

Yes, Captain?

CARBON

Since all the men of my company are here, please introduce
them to the Count.

CYRANO

(*Taking two steps toward* DE GUICHE *and pointing to
the* CADETS)
These are the stouthearted Gascon Cadets
Of Carbon de Castel-Jaloux;
They fight over trifles and shamelessly lie;
These are the stouthearted Gascon Cadets!
Their knowledge of heraldry can't be surpassed;
No plowman can claim nobler birth;
These are the stouthearted Gascon Cadets
Of Carbon de Castel-Jaloux.

Keen-eyed as eagles and fiercer than wolves,
With the elegant grace of a cat,
They sweep all before them, wherever they go,
Keen-eyed as eagles and fiercer than wolves,
Wearing their battered old hats jauntily,
With feathers to cover the holes,
Keen-eyed as eagles and fiercer than wolves,
With the elegant grace of a cat.

Skull-Breaker, Cutthroat, Gut-Sticker, and Slash
Are the most peaceful nicknames they bear;
A passion for glory obsesses them all,

Skull-Breaker, Cutthroat, Gut-Sticker, and Slash
Wherever there's brawling, you'll find them on hand,
Each doing his share, and much more;
Skull-Breaker, Cutthroat, Gut-Sticker, and Slash
Are the most peaceful nicknames they bear.

These are the stouthearted Gascon Cadets
Who cuckold young husbands and old;
Adorable ladies, your virtue is doomed,
These are the stouthearted Gascon Cadets!
Your jealous defenders may grumble and scowl,
They're powerless to alter their fate;
These are the stouthearted Gascon Cadets
Who cuckold young husbands and old.

DE GUICHE
(*Casually seated in an armchair that* RAGUENEAU *has quickly brought for him*)
Poets are a fashionable luxury these days. Would you like to become one of my followers?

CYRANO
No, sir, I prefer to follow no one.

DE GUICHE
My uncle, Cardinal Richelieu, was amused by your dashing combat yesterday. I'm willing to help you with him, if you like.

LE BRET
(*Dazzled*)
My God!

DE GUICHE
You've written a play, I believe....

LE BRET
(*Aside, to* CYRANO)
Your *Agrippine** will soon be performed, my friend!

DE GUICHE
Take it to him.

CYRANO
(*Tempted and rather pleased*)
Really, I...

DE GUICHE
He knows a great deal about the theater. He'll rewrite a few lines....

* *La Mort d'Agrippine* is a play written by the real Cyrano.

CYRANO
(*Whose face has immediately darkened*)
Impossible, sir; my blood curdles at the thought of having a single comma changed.

DE GUICHE
But when a piece of writing pleases him, he pays very well for it.

CYRANO
He couldn't pay as well as I do. When I write something that I like, I reward the author by reciting it to myself.

DE GUICHE
You're a proud man.

CYRANO
Have you noticed that?
(*A* CADET *enters, holding his sword aloft to display the hats that are spitted on it. They are all shabby and misshapen, with bedraggled plumes.*)

THE CADET
Look, Cyrano, at the strange feathered game we took in the street this morning! The men you routed seem to have run away too fast for their hats to follow them!

CARBON
The spoils of war!

EVERYONE
(*Laughing*)
Ha! ha! ha!

CUIGY
The man who hired those cowardly brutes must be in a rage today!

BRISSAILLE
Do you know who did it?

DE GUICHE
I did. (*The laughter ceases.*) I hired them for a task that one doesn't do oneself: punishing a drunken rhymester.
(*Uncomfortable silence*)

THE CADET
(*Aside, to* CYRANO, *showing him the hats*)
What shall we do with these? They're greasy—shall we make them into a stew?
(CYRANO *takes the sword on which the hats are spitted and lowers it in a gesture of homage to* DE GUICHE, *making them all slide off onto the floor at his feet.*)

CYRANO

Sir, would you like to take these back to your friends?

DE GUICHE

(*In a peremptory tone, standing up*)
Bring my sedan chair immediately. I'm leaving. (*To* CYRANO, *violently*) You, sir! . . .

A VOICE

(*Shouting, from outside*)
Porters! Bring Monsieur de Guiche's chair!

DE GUICHE

(*With a smile, having regained his self-control*)
Have you read *Don Quixote?*

CYRANO

Yes, I have, and I take off my hat to you in the name of that scatterbrained hero.

DE GUICHE

You would do well to meditate . . .

A PORTER

(*Appearing in the background*)
The sedan chair is here.

DE GUICHE

. . . on the chapter concerning windmills.

CYRANO

(*Bowing*)
Chapter Thirteen.

DE GUICHE

Because when one attacks them . . .

CYRANO

Do you mean to say that I attack people who veer with every change of wind?

DE GUICHE

When one attacks them, their great arms often hurl one down into the mud!

CYRANO

Or up into the stars!
(DE GUICHE *leaves. He is seen getting into his sedan chair. The* OFFICERS *walk away, whispering to one another.* LE BRET *accompanies them to the door. The* CROWD *leaves.*)

Scene VIII

Cyrano, Le Bret, the Cadets, who are seated at tables to left and right and are being served food and drink.

CYRANO

(Mockingly bowing to those who are leaving without daring to bid him good-by)
Gentlemen. . . . Gentlemen. . . . Gentlemen. . . .

LE BRET

(Coming back from the door and throwing up his arms in despair)
This time you've outdone yourself!

CYRANO

Must I listen to your complaining again?

LE BRET

You shatter every opportunity that comes your way! You'll have to admit that you go too far!

CYRANO

Yes, I go too far.

LE BRET

(Triumphantly)
You *do* admit it!

CYRANO

But for the sake of principle, and to set an example, too, I feel that it's good to go too far in that direction.

LE BRET

If you would only soften your haughty spirit a little, fortune and glory would . . .

CYRANO

But what would I have to do? Cover myself with the protection of some powerful patron? Imitate the ivy that licks the bark of a tall tree while entwining itself around its trunk, and make my way upward by guile, rather than climbing by my own strength? No, thank you. Dedicate poems to financiers, as so many others do? Change myself into a buffoon in the hope of seeing a minister give me a condescending smile? No, thank you. Swallow insults every day? Crawl till the skin of my belly is rubbed raw? Dirty my knees and make my spine as limber as an eel's? No, thank you. Develop the art of sitting on both sides of a

87

fence at once? Pay for an ounce of favor with a ton of flattery? No, thank you. Use women as stepping-stones? Make headway in the sea of life with madrigals for oars and the sighs of old ladies for the wind in my sails? No, thank you. Have poetry published at my own expense? No, thank you. Attend councils held in taverns by imbeciles, trying to win the honor of being chosen as their pope? No, thank you. Work to make a name for myself with one son-net, instead of writing others? No, thank you. See talent only in nonentities? Be terrified of the gazettes, and con-stantly be thinking, "Oh, if only the *Mercure François* will say a kind word about me?" No, thank you. Be always scheming and afraid of schemes? Like paying visits better than writing poetry? Make humble requests? Seek introduc-tions to useful people? No, thank you! No! No! I prefer to lead a different kind of life. I sing, dream, laugh, and go where I please, alone and free. My eyes see clearly and my voice is strong. I'm quarrelsome or benign as it suits my pleasure, always ready to fight a duel or write a poem at the drop of a hat. I dream of flying to the moon but give no thought to fame or fortune. I write only what comes out of myself, and I make it my modest rule to be satisfied with whatever flowers, fruit, or even leaves I gather, as long as they're from my own garden. Then if I should happen to gain some small success I'm not obliged to render any of it unto Caesar. In short, I scorn to be like parasitic ivy, even though I'm not an oak. I may not rise very high, but I'll climb alone!

LE BRET

Be alone if you like, but why have everyone against you? How the devil did you acquire that appalling mania for making enemies wherever you go?

CYRANO

I acquired it by watching others make multitudes of friends and laugh at them behind their backs! I like to exchange as few greetings as possible when I go out, and I'm always glad to add another enemy to my list.

LE BRET

Sheer perversity!

CYRANO

Let's call it my vice. It pleases me to displease. I love to be hated. If you only knew how stimulating it is to be under the murderous fire of hostile eyes, and how amusing it is to watch faces turn venomous with envy or sweaty

with fear! The soft friendship that surrounds others is like
one of those loose, floating Italian collars that leave your
neck free to bend in all directions: you're more comfort-
able, but your head is less erect. But the hatred that presses
in upon me is like a starched Spanish ruff whose stiffness
forces me to hold my head high. Each new enemy is a
pleat that constrains me still more, yet adds to my splendor,
because hatred is both a yoke and a halo of glory!

LE BRET
(*After a silence, passing his arm under* CYRANO'*s*)
Proclaim your pride and bitterness loudly to the world,
but to me speak softly and tell me simply that she doesn't
love you.

CYRANO
(*Sharply*)
Stop! Enough!
(CHRISTIAN *has entered some time earlier and mingled
with the* CADETS, *who have not spoken to him. He has
finally sat down alone at a small table where* LISE *is now
serving him.*)

Scene IX

Cyrano, Le Bret, the Cadets, Christian de Neuvillette.

A CADET
(*Seated at a table upstage, with a glass in his hand*)
Cyrano! (CYRANO *looks around.*) Will you tell us your
story now?

CYRANO
Not now. A little later.
(*He and* LE BRET *walk upstage, arm in arm, talking
quietly together.*)

THE CADET
(*Standing up and coming downstage*)
The story of Cyrano's combat will be the best lesson . . .
(*Stops at* CHRISTIAN'*s table.*) . . . for this timid apprentice.

CHRISTIAN
(*Looking up*)
Apprentice?

ANOTHER CADET

Yes, you sickly northerner.

CHRISTIAN

Sickly?

FIRST CADET

(*Banteringly*)
Monsieur de Neuvillette, it's time for you to learn something. There's a certain object that we all avoid naming as scrupulously as we would refrain from mentioning rope in the house of a man whose father had been hanged.

CHRISTIAN

What is it?

THIRD CADET

(*With majestic authority*)
Look at me! (*Puts his finger to his nose three times, mysteriously.*) Do you understand?

CHRISTIAN

I think so. You must mean . . .

FOURTH CADET

Sh! You must never speak that word! (*Points to* CYRANO, *who is still talking upstage with* LE BRET.) If you do, you'll have *him* to deal with!

FIFTH CADET

(*Who has silently sat down on* CHRISTIAN's *table while his head was turned toward the others*)
He's already killed two men because they had nasal voices!

SIXTH CADET

(*In a hollow tone, standing up after having crawled under the table*)
The slightest allusion to that protuberance brings an untimely death!

SEVENTH CADET

(*Putting his hand on* CHRISTIAN's *shoulder*)
One word is enough! Even a gesture! If you take out your handkerchief, you've taken out your shroud!
(*Silence. The* CADETS *are all around* CHRISTIAN, *looking at him with their arms folded. He stands up and goes to* CARBON DE CASTEL-JALOUX, *who is talking with an* OFFICER *and seems unaware of what has been taking place.*)

CHRISTIAN

Captain!

CARBON
(Turning around and looking him up and down)
Yes?

CHRISTIAN
What should one do when southerners become too boastful?

CARBON
Prove to them that a northerner can be courageous.
(Turns his back on CHRISTIAN.)

CHRISTIAN
Thank you.

FIRST CADET
(To CYRANO)
Now tell us your story!

ALL
Your story!

CYRANO
(Comes toward them.)
My story? . . . *(They all draw up their stools and group themselves around him, straining their necks forward. CHRISTIAN has straddled a chair.)* Well, I was walking alone to meet them. The moon was gleaming like a big silver watch in the sky when suddenly some heavenly hand slipped it into a pocket of clouds. The sky was black as pitch and there were no lights in the street. I couldn't see . . .

CHRISTIAN
Beyond the end of your nose.
(Silence. The CADETS all stand up slowly, looking at CYRANO in terror. He has stopped short, dumbfounded. Several moments of tense waiting go by before he finally speaks.)

CYRANO
Who is this man?

A CADET
(In a low voice)
He came to us only this morning.

CYRANO
(Taking a step toward CHRISTIAN)
This morning?

CARBON

(In a low voice)
His name is Baron de Neuvil—

CYRANO

(Quickly, stopping)
Oh! *(His face takes on an expression of shock, then anger,
and he makes a movement as though to attack* CHRISTIAN.)
I . . . *(He controls himself and speaks dully.)* Very well.
. . . As I was saying . . . *(With a burst of rage in his voice)*
Mordious! *(Continues in a natural tone.)* It was so dark
that I couldn't see anything. *(The* CADETS *are amazed.
They sit down again, staring at him.)* I walked on, think-
ing that for the sake of a poor drunkard I was about to
anger some powerful nobleman who would surely . . .

CHRISTIAN

Resent your nosiness.
(The CADETS *all stand up again.* CHRISTIAN *tilts his
chair.)*

CYRANO

(Choking)
. . . who would surely bear a grudge against me, and that
I was rashly putting . . .

CHRISTIAN

Your nose into . . .

CYRANO

. . . myself into a bad situation, because that nobleman
might . . .

CHRISTIAN

Look down his nose at you.

CYRANO

(Wiping sweat from his forehead)
. . . be able to make things a bit difficult for me. But I said
to myself, "Come, Gascon, do what has to be done. On-
ward, Cyrano!" A moment later, someone . . .

CHRISTIAN

Nosed you out in the darkness.

CYRANO

. . . lunged at me with his sword. I parried the thrust and
suddenly found myself . . .

CHRISTIAN

Nose to nose . . .

CYRANO

(*Rushing toward him*)
No! By all the saints in heaven, I'll . . . (*The Gascons
crowd forward to see better, but as soon as he is in front
of* CHRISTIAN *he again controls himself and continues his
story.*) I found myself facing a hundred shouting brutes,
all smelling . . .

CHRISTIAN

With their noses, of course.

CYRANO

(*Smiling wanly*)
. . . of onions and cheap wine. I plunged into the midst of
them . . .

CHRISTIAN

Nose first!

CYRANO

. . . and immediately cut down two of them. As I was
attacking a third, I saw a sword . . .

CHRISTIAN

Right under your nose!

CYRANO

(*Bellowing*)
Out! All of you! Get out!
(*The* CADETS *all hurry toward the doors.*)

FIRST CADET

The tiger has finally awakened!

CYRANO

Leave me alone with this man!

SECOND CADET

He'll soon be turned into mincemeat!

RAGUENEAU

Mincemeat?

THIRD CADET

Yes, ready to be baked in one of your pie crusts!

RAGUENEAU

I feel faint, and limp as a napkin!

CARBON

Let's go.

FOURTH CADET

There won't be anything left of him!

FIFTH CADET

It makes me tremble just to think of what's going to happen to him!

SIXTH CADET

(*Closing the door on the right as he goes out*)
It will be something horrifying!
(*They have all left, most of them through the doors at the sides and in the background, with a few having disappeared up the stairs.* CHRISTIAN *and* CYRANO *are left standing face to face. They look at each other for a moment.*)

Scene X

Cyrano, Christian.

CYRANO

Embrace me!

CHRISTIAN

Sir . . .

CYRANO

You're a brave man.

CHRISTIAN

Perhaps, but . . .

CYRANO

Very brave. I'm glad to know that.

CHRISTIAN

Would you mind telling me . . .

CYRANO

Embrace me. I'm her brother.

CHRISTIAN

Whose brother?

CYRANO

Hers!

CHRISTIAN

Hers?

CYRANO

Roxane's!

CHRISTIAN

(*Hurrying toward him*)
Oh! You? Her brother?

CYRANO

Yes, or almost. A brotherly cousin.

CHRISTIAN

And she's told you . . .

CYRANO

Everything!

CHRISTIAN

Does she love me?

CYRANO

Perhaps!

CHRISTIAN

(*Taking his hands*)
How happy I am to know you!

CYRANO

That's a rather sudden change of feeling.

CHRISTIAN

Forgive me. . . .

CYRANO

(*Looks at him and puts his hands on his shoulders.*)
It's true: you *are* a handsome devil!

CHRISTIAN

If you only knew, sir, how much I admire you!

CYRANO

But all those "noses" you gave me . . .

CHRISTIAN

I take them all back!

CYRANO

Roxane expects to receive a letter from you this evening.

CHRISTIAN

Oh, no!

CYRANO

What? . . .

CHRISTIAN

If I write to her, she'll never want to see me again.

CYRANO

Why?

CHRISTIAN

Because I'm such a fool that I could die of shame!

CYRANO

No, you're not, since you've said it yourself. Besides, you didn't attack me like a fool.

CHRISTIAN

Words come easily to anyone when he wants to pick a quarrel. I may have a certain quick, soldierly wit, but with women I'm always at a loss for anything to say. Their eyes show interest when I pass by, but . . .

CYRANO

Aren't their hearts also interested when you stop?

CHRISTIAN

No! It's all too clear to me that I'm one of those men who don't know how to speak of love.

CYRANO

I have the feeling that if my features had been shaped more harmoniously, I would have been one of those men who *do* know how to speak of love.

CHRISTIAN

Ah, if only I could express myself gracefully!

CYRANO

If only I had a handsome face!

CHRISTIAN

Roxane is so elegant and refined—I'm sure to disillusion her!

CYRANO

(*Looking at* CHRISTIAN)

If I had such an interpreter to speak for my soul . . .

CHRISTIAN

(*Despairingly*)

I need eloquence, and I have none!

CYRANO

(*Abruptly*)

I'll lend you mine! Lend me your conquering physical charm, and together we'll form a romantic hero!

CHRISTIAN

What do you mean?

CYRANO

Do you feel capable of repeating what I tell you every day?

CHRISTIAN

Are you suggesting . . .

CYRANO

Roxane won't be disillusioned! Together, we can win her heart! Will you let my soul pass from my leather jerkin and lodge beneath your embroidered doublet?

CHRISTIAN

But Cyrano . . .

CYRANO

Are you willing?

CHRISTIAN

You frighten me!

CYRANO

Your only fear is that you'll chill her heart when you speak to her, but if she hears my words from your lips, she'll soon be aflame!

CHRISTIAN

Your eyes are shining. . . .

CYRANO

Will you do it?

CHRISTIAN

Would it please you so much?

CYRANO

(*Ardently*)
It would . . . (*Restrains himself and adopts a more detached tone.*) It would amuse me! It's an experiment that would tempt any poet. Shall we complete each other? We'll walk together: you in the light, I in the shadows. I'll make you eloquent, you'll make me handsome.

CHRISTIAN

But I must write her a letter without delay! I'll never be able to . . .

CYRANO

(*Taking out the letter he has written*)
Here's your letter!

CHRISTIAN

What . . .

CYRANO

It lacks only the name and address.

CHRISTIAN

I . . .

CYRANO

You can send it as it is. Don't worry, it's well written.

CHRISTIAN

Had you already . . .

CYRANO

I always have a letter in my pocket, written to some imaginary lady, because I'm one of those men whose only sweethearts are dreams breathed into the bubble of a name. You can change my fantasy to reality. You can take my vows and pleas, launched at random into the empty air, and give them all a single destination. You'll see that in this letter my feelings are all the better expressed for being insincere! Here, take it.

CHRISTIAN

Won't some things in it have to be changed? Since you wrote it with no specific woman in mind, how can it fit Roxane?

CYRANO

It will fit her like a glove!

CHRISTIAN

But . . .

CYRANO

You can count on vanity to make her think it was written for her!

CHRISTIAN

Ah, my friend! . . .
(*He throws himself into* CYRANO's *arms. They stand embracing each other.*)

Scene XI

Cyrano, Christian, the Gascons, the Musketeer, Lise.

A CADET
(*Pushing the door ajar*)
Nothing. . . . A deathly silence. . . . I'm afraid to look. . . .
(*Puts his head through the doorway.*) What!

ALL THE CADETS
(*Entering and seeing* CYRANO *and* CHRISTIAN *embracing each other*)
Oh!—Ah!

A CADET
I can't believe my eyes!
(*Consternation*)

THE MUSKETEER
(*Jeeringly*)
Well, look at that!

CARBON
Our demon has become as gentle as a lamb! When he's struck on one nostril, he turns the other!

THE MUSKETEER
He lets people talk about his nose now? (*Calls out to* LISE, *with a triumphant expression.*) Lise! Watch this! (*Approaches* CYRANO *and insolently stares at his nose.*) What's that long thing on your face, sir? It reminds me of something, but I can't recall what it is.

CYRANO
Then let me help you by jarring your memory!
(*Slaps him. The* CADETS *are delighted to see* CYRANO *behaving like himself again. They caper joyfully.*)

CURTAIN

ACT THREE

Roxane's Kiss

A little square in the Marais quarter of Paris. Old houses and a perspective of narrow streets. To the right, ROXANE's *house and the wall of its garden, overflowing with foliage. Above the door, a window and a balcony. A bench in front of the threshold.*

Ivy on the wall. The balcony is garlanded with quivering, drooping jasmine.

By means of the bench and the jutting stones of the wall, one can easily climb up to the balcony.

Opposite, another old house in the same style, made of brick and stone, with an entrance door. The knocker of this door is wrapped in cloth like an injured thumb.

As the curtain rises, the DUENNA *is seated on the bench. The window is open wide onto* ROXANE's *balcony.*

Beside the DUENNA *stands* RAGUENEAU, *dressed in a kind of livery. He is finishing a story, and wiping his eyes.*

Scene I

Ragueneau, the Duenna, then Roxane, Cyrano, and two Pages.

100

RAGUENEAU

... and then she ran off with a musketeer! Alone and ruined, I felt I had nothing to live for, so I tried to hang myself, but Monsieur de Bergerac came in and cut me down. Then he offered me this position as his cousin's steward.

THE DUENNA

But how did you come to be ruined?

RAGUENEAU

Lise liked warriors and I liked poets. Mars ate everything that Apollo left. At that rate, it didn't take long!

THE DUENNA

(*Standing up and calling toward the open window*)
Roxane, are you ready? We're late!

ROXANE'S VOICE

(*From the window*)
I'm just putting on my cloak!

THE DUENNA

(*To* RAGUENEAU, *pointing to the door opposite*)
That's where we're going, to Clomire's. She holds regular discussion meetings in her house. A discourse on the Tender Passion will be read today.

RAGUENEAU

The Tender Passion?

THE DUENNA

(*Simpering*)
Yes, that's right. (*Shouts toward the window.*) Roxane! Hurry or we'll miss the discourse on the Tender Passion!

ROXANE'S VOICE

I'm coming!
(*A sound of stringed instruments is heard approaching.*)

CYRANO'S VOICE

(*Singing offstage*)
La-la-la-la ...

THE DUENNA

(*Surprised*)
Is someone coming to play for us?

CYRANO

(*Entering, followed by two* PAGES *carrying lutes*)
Those are thirty-second notes, you fool!

FIRST PAGE

(*Ironically*)
Ah, so you know about thirty-second notes, sir!

CYRANO

I'm a musician, like all of Gassendi's* disciples!

THE PAGE

(*Playing and singing*)
La-la . . .

CYRANO

(*Takes the lute away from him and continues the melody.*)
Let me do it! La-la-la-la . . .

ROXANE

(*Appearing on the balcony*)
Ah, it's you!

CYRANO

(*Singing his words to the melody*)
I've come to salute your lilies, and pay my respects to your roses!

ROXANE

I'm coming down!
(*Leaves the balcony.*)

THE DUENNA

(*Pointing to the* PAGES)
Where did these two virtuosi come from?

CYRANO

I won them from d'Assoucy on a bet. We were arguing about a point of grammar when suddenly he pointed to these lute-playing louts, who always accompany him wherever he goes, and said to me, "I'll bet you a day of music!" He lost, and therefore ordered them to follow me and bear harmonious witness to everything I do until tomorrow. It was charming at first, but it has already begun to pall. (*To*

* Pierre Gassendi (1592–1655), French mathematician and philosopher. The real Cyrano is said to have studied with him, but there is no certain evidence of it.

the PAGES) Go and serenade Montfleury, and tell him I
sent you! (*The* PAGES *go upstage to leave.* CYRANO *turns
back to the* DUENNA.) I've come to ask Roxane, as I do
every day . . . (*To the* PAGES, *as they are leaving*) Play a
long time—and off-key! (*To the* DUENNA) . . . whether
her soulmate is still a model of perfection.

ROXANE
(*Coming out of the house*)
Oh, he's so handsome! And such a brilliant mind! I can't
tell you how much I love him!

CYRANO
(*Smiling*)
You feel that Christian has a brilliant mind?

ROXANE
Even more brilliant than yours!

CYRANO
I won't contest that.

ROXANE
I don't believe there's anyone in the world who can
match him in saying those sweet nothings that mean everything. Sometimes he seems distracted and his inspiration
falters, then all at once he says exquisite things to me!

CYRANO
(*Incredulously*)
Really?

ROXANE
Just like a man! Because he's handsome, you think he has
to be dull-witted!

CYRANO
Does he speak well about matters of the heart?

ROXANE
Not well—superbly!

CYRANO
And how does he write?

ROXANE
Even better than he speaks! Just listen to this! (*Declaiming*)
"The more you take of my heart, the more I have!" (*Tri-
umphantly*) There, what do you think of that?

CYRANO
(*Unenthusiastically*)
Oh . . .

ROXANE
And this: "Since I need a heart with which to suffer, if you keep mine, send me yours!"

CYRANO
First he has too much heart, then not enough. He can't seem to make up his mind.

ROXANE
(*Stamping her foot*)
You're exasperating! You only talk like that because you're jealous . . .

CYRANO
(*Starting*)
What?

ROXANE
. . . of the way he writes! Listen to this and tell me if you think anything could be more tender: "Believe me when I say that my heart cries out to you, and that if kisses could be sent in writing, you would read this letter with your lips."

CYRANO
(*Smiling with satisfaction in spite of himself*)
Well, those lines are . . . (*Catches himself and continues in a disdainful tone.*) . . . rather affected.

ROXANE
And listen to this. . . .

CYRANO
(*Delighted*)
You know all his letters by heart?

ROXANE
Every one of them!

CYRANO
(*Twisting his mustache*)
That's quite flattering.

ROXANE
He's a master of eloquence!

CYRANO

(*Modestly*)
Let's not exaggerate. . . .

ROXANE

(*Peremptorily*)
A master!

CYRANO

(*Bowing*)
Very well, then, a master!

THE DUENNA
(*Hurrying downstage, after having gone upstage earlier*)
Monsieur de Guiche is coming! (*To* CYRANO, *pushing him toward the house*) Go inside! It will be better for him not to find you here; it might put him on the scent. . . .

ROXANE

(*To* CYRANO)
Yes, on the scent of my precious secret! He's in love with me and he's powerful—he mustn't know! He might strike a cruel blow at my love for Christian!

CYRANO

(*Entering the house*)
I'll do as you wish.
     (DE GUICHE *appears.*)

Scene II

Roxane, De Guiche, the Duenna in the background.

ROXANE
(*To* DE GUICHE, *with a curtsey*)
We were about to leave. . . .

DE GUICHE
I've come to say good-by.

ROXANE
You're going away?

DE GUICHE
Yes. To war.

ROXANE

Ah!

DE GUICHE

I'm leaving tonight.

ROXANE

Ah!

DE GUICHE

I have my orders. We're besieging Arras.*

ROXANE

Ah! A siege?

DE GUICHE

Yes. . . . My departure seems to leave you cold.

ROXANE

(*Politely*)
Not at all.

DE GUICHE

For my part, I'm heartbroken. Will I ever see you again?
If so, when? . . . Do you know that I've been made a
colonel?

ROXANE

(*With indifference*)
Congratulations.

DE GUICHE

And I'm in command of the Guards.

ROXANE

(*Startled*)
The Guards?

DE GUICHE

Yes, the regiment in which your boastful cousin serves.
I'll find a way to take revenge on him when we're at Arras.

ROXANE

(*Choking*)
What! The Guards are being sent there?

DE GUICHE

(*Laughing*)
Of course: that's my regiment.
(ROXANE *sits down heavily on the bench.*)

* A city, now in France, which was captured by the French from
the Spanish in 1640, when it was part of the Spanish Netherlands.

ROXANE

(Aside)
Christian! . . .

DE GUICHE

What's the matter?

ROXANE

(Overwhelmed with emotion)
I'm in despair at . . . at what you've told me. . . . When a woman cares for a man and learns that he's going to war . . .

DE GUICHE

(Surprised and delighted)
Why did you wait for the day of my departure to say such a tender thing to me for the first time?

ROXANE

(Changing her tone and fanning herself)
So you're going to take revenge on my cousin?

DE GUICHE

(Smiling)
Do you side with him?

ROXANE

No—against him!

DE GUICHE

Do you see him?

ROXANE

Very seldom.

DE GUICHE

He's seen everywhere with one of the Cadets . . . *(Tries to think of the name.)* . . . a young man named Neu . . . Neuvillen . . . Neuviller . . .

ROXANE

Tall?

DE GUICHE

Yes, with blond hair.

ROXANE

Reddish blond.

DE GUICHE

And handsome.

ROXANE

Not very.

DE GUICHE

But stupid.

ROXANE

He looks like it. (*Changing her tone*) Are you planning to take revenge on Cyrano by exposing him to the fire of the enemy? If so, you'll get little satisfaction from it, because he loves danger! I know how you could really make him suffer!

DE GUICHE

How?

ROXANE

Leave him behind with his dear Cadets when the regiment goes off to fight. Make him sit idly in Paris through the whole war! That's the best way to torment a man like him. If you want to punish him, deprive him of danger!

DE GUICHE

Only a woman could have thought of a trick like that!

ROXANE

He'll eat his heart out at not being in action, his friends will angrily chew their fingernails, and you'll be avenged.

DE GUICHE

(*Drawing closer*)
Then you do love me a little! (*She smiles.*) I like to think that your sharing my rancor is a sign of love, Roxane!

ROXANE

It is.

DE GUICHE

(*Showing her several sealed envelopes*)
I have orders that will be delivered to each company without delay, except . . . (*Separates one of them from the others.*) . . . for this one, addressed to the Cadets! (*Puts it in his pocket.*) I'll keep it. (*Laughing*) Ha, ha, Cyrano! We'll see how your warlike temperament takes to this! . . . Tell me, Roxane, do you sometimes play tricks on people yourself?

ROXANE

(*Looking at him*)
Yes, sometimes.

DE GUICHE

(*Close to her*)
You drive me mad! I intended to leave tonight, but how can
I part from you when you've just revealed such feelings to
me? Listen. . . . Near here, on the Rue d'Orléans, there's a
monastery founded by the syndic of the Capuchins, Father
Athanare. Laymen aren't allowed to enter it, but I'll see to
it that the good monks make an exception in my case. Their
sleeves are wide enough to let me hide in them! The Capuchins serve Cardinal Richelieu directly; their awe of the
uncle makes them fear the nephew. Everyone will believe
I've left Paris. I'll then come to you, masked. Let me delay
my departure one day!

ROXANE

(*Anxiously*)
But if it becomes known, your glory will be . . .

DE GUICHE

Have no fear!

ROXANE

But the siege of Arras . . .

DE GUICHE

Never mind! Let me do it!

ROXANE

No!

DE GUICHE

Let me!

ROXANE

(*Tenderly*)
I must refuse.

DE GUICHE

Ah!

ROXANE

Go! (*Aside*) And Christian will stay. (*To* DE GUICHE) I
want you to be heroic . . . Antoine!

DE GUICHE
What heavenly words! Do you love . . .

ROXANE
Yes, I love the man for whom I fear.

DE GUICHE

(*Overjoyed*)
I'm going now! (*Kisses her hand.*) Are you satisfied?

ROXANE

Yes, Antoine.
    (*He leaves.*)

THE DUENNA
    (*Bowing comically to him behind his back*)
Yes, Antoine!

ROXANE
    (*To the* DUENNA)
Don't say a word about what I've done. Cyrano would
never forgive me if he knew I'd robbed him of his war!
(*Calls toward the house.*) Cousin!

Scene III

Roxane, the Duenna, Cyrano.

ROXANE
We're going to Clomire's house. (*Points to the door opposite.*) Alcandre and Lysimon are going to speak there!

THE DUENNA
Yes, but something tells me that we're going to miss them.

CYRANO
    (*To* ROXANE)
I wouldn't want you to miss those parrots.
    (*They have arrived in front of* CLOMIRE's *door.*)

THE DUENNA
    (*With delight*)
Oh, look! The knocker is wrapped in cloth! (*To the knocker*)
You've been gagged, you metallic little brute, to prevent
you from disturbing the noble speeches!
    (*Carefully lifts it and knocks gently.*)

ROXANE
    (*Seeing that the door is being opened*)
Let's go inside! (*From the threshold, to* CYRANO) If Christian comes, as I presume he will, tell him to wait for me.

CYRANO
(Quickly, as she is about to disappear)
One moment! *(She turns back toward him.)* You always
have a subject on which you question him; what will it be
this time?

ROXANE

This time ...

CYRANO
(Eagerly)
Yes?

ROXANE

You won't tell him?

CYRANO

I'll be as silent as a tomb.

ROXANE

Well, this time I'm not going to question him about anything! I'll say to him, "Give free rein to your mind! Impro-
vise! Speak to me of love in your magnificent way!"

CYRANO
(Smiling)
Good.

ROXANE

Sh!

CYRANO

Sh!

ROXANE

Not a word!
(Goes inside and closes the door behind her.)

CYRANO
(Bowing to her, after the door is closed)
I thank you.
(The door opens again and ROXANE's *head appears.)*

ROXANE

If he knew, he might prepare a speech in advance!

CYRANO

Do you really think so?

BOTH TOGETHER

Sh!
(The door closes.)

CYRANO

(*Calling*)
Christian!

Scene IV

Cyrano, Christian.

CYRANO

I know what we need to know. Prepare your memory: here's a chance to cover yourself with glory! Why are you looking so unhappy? Come, there's no time to lose! We'll hurry to your house and I'll tell you . . .

CHRISTIAN

No!

CYRANO

What?

CHRISTIAN

No! I'm going to wait for Roxane here.

CYRANO

Have you lost your reason? Come with me, you must learn . . .

CHRISTIAN

No, I tell you! I'm tired of borrowing my letters and speeches, of always playing a part and trembling lest I forget my lines! It was necessary at the beginning and I'm grateful to you for your help, but now that I feel she really loves me, I'm no longer afraid. I'm going to speak for myself.

CYRANO

(*Ironically*)
Do you believe that's a good idea?

CHRISTIAN

What makes you think I can't do it? After all, I'm not so stupid! You'll see! Your lessons haven't been wasted on me, my friend: I'm sure I can speak without your guidance now. And in any case I'll certainly know how to take her in my arms! (*Sees* ROXANE *coming out of* CLOMIRE'S *house.*) Here she comes! No, Cyrano, don't leave me!

CYRANO

(*Bowing to him*)
Speak for yourself, sir.
(*Disappears behind the garden wall.*)

Scene V

ROXANE

Christian, Roxane, and briefly, the Duenna and several intellectual ladies and gentlemen.

(*Coming out of* CLOMIRE's *house with the other guests and exchanging farewell bows with them*)
Good-by, Barthénoïde . . . Alcandre . . . Grémione . . .

THE DUENNA

(*Despairingly*)
We missed the discourse on the Tender Passion!
(*Goes into* ROXANE's *house.*)

ROXANE

(*Still bowing*)
Urimédonte . . . Good-by! (*They all bow to her and to each other, then separate and go off in different directions. She sees* CHRISTIAN.) Ah, it's you! (*Goes to him.*) Dusk is gathering. Wait. . . . They're far away now. The air is pleasant and no one is passing by. Let's sit down. Talk to me. I'm listening.
(CHRISTIAN *sits down beside her on the bench. There is a silence.*)

CHRISTIAN

I love you.

ROXANE

(*Closing her eyes*)
Yes, speak to me of love.

CHRISTIAN

I love you.

ROXANE

That's the theme—now elaborate on it.

CHRISTIAN

I love . . .

ROXANE

Develop your theme!

CHRISTIAN

I love you so much!

ROXANE

Go on.

CHRISTIAN

I . . . I'd be so happy if you loved me! Tell me that you do, Roxane!

ROXANE
  (Pouting)
You're giving me water when I expected cream! Tell me how you love me.

CHRISTIAN

I love you . . . very much!

ROXANE

Surely you can express your feelings better than that!

CHRISTIAN
  (Who has moved closer to her and is now devouring her neck with his eyes)
Your neck! I'd like to kiss it. . . .

ROXANE

Christian!

CHRISTIAN

I love you!

ROXANE
  (Starting to stand up)
Again!

CHRISTIAN
  (Quickly, holding her back)
No, I don't love you!

ROXANE
  (Sitting down again)
At least that's a change.

CHRISTIAN

I adore you!

ROXANE
(*Standing up and moving away*)
Oh!

CHRISTIAN
Yes. . . . I'm becoming foolish!

ROXANE
(*Curtly*)
And it displeases me! As it would displease me if you became ugly.

CHRISTIAN
But . . .

ROXANE
Try to bring back your vanished eloquence!

CHRISTIAN
I . . .

ROXANE
I know: you love me. Good-by.
(*Goes toward the house.*)

CHRISTIAN
Wait! Let me tell you . . .

ROXANE
(*Opening the door*)
That you adore me? I already know that. No, no! Go away!

CHRISTIAN
But I . . .
(*She closes the door in his face.*)

CYRANO
(*Who has returned a short time earlier without being seen*)
Congratulations on your success.

Scene VI

Christian, Cyrano, the Pages briefly.

CHRISTIAN
Help me!

CYRANO

No.

CHRISTIAN

If I don't win her back immediately, I'll die!

CYRANO

How the devil do you expect me to teach you immediately . . .

CHRISTIAN

(Gripping his arm)
Oh! Look!
(A light has appeared in the balcony window.)

CYRANO

(With deep emotion)
Her window!

CHRISTIAN

(Shouting)
I'll die!

CYRANO

Lower your voice!

CHRISTIAN

(Softly)
I'll die. . . .

CYRANO

It's dark now.

CHRISTIAN

What of it?

CYRANO

The damage can be repaired. You don't deserve . . . Stand here, in front of the balcony, you wretched fool! I'll be under it, telling you what to say.

CHRISTIAN

But . . .

CYRANO

Quiet!
(The PAGES appear in the background.)

THE PAGES

(*To* CYRANO)
Here we are!

CYRANO

Sh!
(*Signals them to speak softly.*)

FIRST PAGE

(*In an undertone*)
We've been serenading Montfleury!

CYRANO

(*Quickly, also in an undertone*)
I want you to stand watch, one at that corner, the other at that one. If you see anyone coming, begin playing your lutes.

SECOND PAGE

What shall we play, noble disciple of Gassendi?

CYRANO

A happy melody for a woman, a sad one for a man. (*The* PAGES *disappear, one toward each street corner.* CYRANO *speaks to* CHRISTIAN.) Call her!

CHRISTIAN

Roxane!

CYRANO

(*Picking up pebbles and throwing them against the window*)
Just a moment. First, a few pebbles. . . .

Scene VII

Roxane, Christian, Cyrano, hidden at first under the balcony.

ROXANE

(*Partially opening her window*)
Who's there?

CHRISTIAN

It's I.

ROXANE

Who?

CHRISTIAN

Christian.

ROXANE
    (*With disdain*)
Oh, it's you.

CHRISTIAN

I'd like to speak to you.

CYRANO
    (*Under the balcony, to* CHRISTIAN)
That's good. Keep your voice down.

ROXANE

No! You speak too awkwardly. Go away.

CHRISTIAN

Please. . . .

ROXANE

No! You've stopped loving me!

CHRISTIAN
    (*Repeating what* CYRANO *tells him*)
Impossible! . . . I could no more . . . stop loving you . . .
than I could stop . . . the rising of the sun!

ROXANE
    (*Pausing just as she was about to close the window*)
Ah! That's better!

CHRISTIAN
    (*Still repeating* CYRANO'*s words*)
My cruel love . . . has never ceased to grow . . . in my tor-
mented soul . . . since the day . . . when it was born there.

ROXANE
    (*Coming out onto the balcony*)
That's better! . . . But since your love is cruel, you were
foolish not to smother it at birth.

CHRISTIAN
    (*Still repeating*)
I tried, without success. . . . It had the strength of Hercu-
les . . . from the first moment of its life.

ROXANE

That's better!

CHRISTIAN

(*Still repeating*)
And so it strangled . . . without effort . . . the two ser-
pents . . . of Pride and Doubt.

ROXANE

(*Leaning forward with her elbows on the railing of the
balcony*)
Very good! . . . But why do you speak so haltingly? Has
your imagination gone lame?

CYRANO

(*Pulling* CHRISTIAN *under the balcony and taking his
place*)
Sh! This is becoming too difficult!

ROXANE

Your words are hesitant tonight. Why?

CYRANO

(*Speaking softly, like* CHRISTIAN)
Because of the darkness, they must grope their way to your
ears.

ROXANE

My words have no such difficulty.

CYRANO

They go straight to my heart, a goal too large to miss,
whereas your ears are small. And your words travel swiftly
because they fall, while mine must slowly climb.

ROXANE

But they seem to be climbing better now.

CYRANO

They've finally become accustomed to that exercise.

ROXANE

It's true that I'm speaking from high above you.

CYRANO

Yes, and it would kill me if you let a harsh word fall on my
heart from that height!

ROXANE

(*Making a movement*)
I'll come down to you!

CYRANO

(*Urgently*)
No!

ROXANE
(*Pointing to the bench below the balcony*)
Then climb up on that bench.

CYRANO
(*Stepping back into the shadows in alarm*)
No!

ROXANE
Why not?

CYRANO
(*Increasingly overcome by emotion*)
I want to go on taking advantage of this opportunity . . .
this chance for us to talk quietly . . . without seeing each
other.

ROXANE
Why should we talk without seeing each other?

CYRANO
I find it delightful. We're almost invisible to each other.
You see the blackness of a long cloak, I see the whiteness
of a summer dress. I'm only a shadow, you're only a spot of
brightness. You can't know what these moments mean to
me! I may sometimes have been eloquent in the past . . .

ROXANE
You have!

CYRANO
. . . but until now my words have never come from my true
heart.

ROXANE
Why?

CYRANO
Because . . . till now I always spoke through . . .

ROXANE
Through what?

CYRANO
The intoxication that seizes anyone who stands before your
gaze! . . . But tonight it seems to me that I'm speaking to
you for the first time.

ROXANE
Perhaps it's true—even your voice is different.

CYRANO
(*Impetuously moving closer*)
Yes, quite different, because in the protecting darkness I

dare at last to be myself, I dare . . . (*Pauses, then continues distractedly.*) What was I saying? I don't know. . . . All this . . . Excuse my agitation! All this is so enchanting . . . so new to me!

ROXANE

So new?

CYRANO

(*Deeply stirred, and still trying to cover up what he has admitted*)
Yes, it's new to me to be sincere . . . without fear of being laughed at. . . .

ROXANE

Laughed at for what?

CYRANO

For . . . for an outburst of feeling! My heart always timidly hides itself behind my mind. I set out to bring down stars from the sky, then, for fear of ridicule, I stop and pick little flowers of eloquence.

ROXANE

Those little flowers have their charm.

CYRANO

Yes, but let's scorn them tonight!

ROXANE

You've never talked to me like this before.

CYRANO

I'd like to turn away from Cupid and his arrows, and go with you toward . . . fresher things! Rather than daintily sipping stale sentimentality from ornate golden cups, let's try to learn how the soul slakes its thirst by drinking directly from the great river of love!

ROXANE

But you yourself . . .

CYRANO

Yes, I used pretty phrases at first, to make you listen to me, but now it would be an insult to this fragrant night, this moment, and nature herself, if I were to speak with the affected elegance of a courtly love letter! One look at the starry sky above us is enough to make me want to throw off all artificiality. If the expression of feeling is refined too much, the feeling itself is lost. The soul is emptied by such vain pastimes, and love dies, smothered under a mass of flowery words that were meant to embellish it.

ROXANE

But it seems to me that elegant language . . .

CYRANO

It has no place in true love! It's only a game, and those who love will suffer if they play it too long. For most of them there comes a time—and I pity those for whom it doesn't come!—when they feel a noble love inside themselves that's saddened by every grandiloquent word they say.

ROXANE

Well, if that time has come for us, what words will you say to me?

CYRANO

All those that enter my mind of their own accord. I'll give them to you as they come, without arranging them in bouquets: I love you, I'm overwhelmed, I love you to the point of madness! Your name is in my heart like a bell shaken by my constant trembling, ringing day and night: Roxane, Roxane, Roxane! Loving everything about you, I forget nothing. I remember the day last year, the twelfth of May, when you wore your hair in a different style. Just as a man who has looked at the sun too long sees red circles everywhere, when I've gazed on the bright glory of your hair my dazzled eyes see golden spots on everything!

ROXANE

(*In a tremulous voice*)
Yes, that's really love. . . .

CYRANO

Of course! The feeling that holds me in its merciless grip could be nothing else but love! It has all the terrible jealousy and somber violence of love, and all the unselfishness, too. How gladly I would give my happiness for the sake of yours, even without your knowledge, asking only to hear from a distance, now and then, the laughter born of my sacrifice! Each time I look at you, you strengthen my courage and bring forth some new virtue. Are you beginning to understand now? Do you feel my soul rising to you in the darkness? Ah, it's all too beautiful, too sweet, this evening! I say all these things and you listen to me—*you* listen to *me*! It's more than my poor heart can bear! Even in my most daring dreams I never hoped for so much! I could die happily at this moment! It's because of my words that you're trembling—for you *are* trembling, like one of the

leaves in the dark foliage above me: I've felt the beloved
tremor of your hand descending along the jasmine branches!
(*Fervently kisses the end of a drooping branch.*)

ROXANE

Yes, I'm trembling, and I'm weeping, and I love you, and
I'm yours! You've made me drunk with love!

CYRANO

Then let death come, now that I've aroused such feelings
in you! I ask only one thing . . .

CHRISTIAN

(*From under the balcony*)
A kiss!

ROXANE

(*Quickly drawing back*)
What?

CYRANO

Oh!

ROXANE

You ask . . .

CYRANO

Yes, I . . . (*To* CHRISTIAN, *in an undertone*) You're going
too fast!

CHRISTIAN

She's in a willing mood—I must take advantage of it!

CYRANO

(*To* ROXANE)
Yes, I . . . I asked for a kiss, but I now realize that I was
much too bold.

ROXANE

(*A little disappointed*)
You don't insist?

CYRANO

Yes, I insist . . . but not insistently! I've offended your modesty. . . . Don't give me that kiss!

CHRISTIAN

(*To* CYRANO, *tugging at his cloak*)
Why do you say that?

CYRANO

Quiet, Christian!

ROXANE

(*Leaning forward*)
What are you saying?

CYRANO

I was scolding myself for having gone too far. I just said to
myself, "Quiet, Christian!" (*The lutes begin playing.*) Wait!
Someone's coming! (ROXANE *closes the window.* CYRANO *lis-
tens to the lutes: one of them is playing gaily, the other
mournfully.*) A sad tune and a happy one, both at the same
time? What do they mean? Is it a man or a woman? . . . Ah!
It's a Capuchin!
    (*A* CAPUCHIN *enters; holding a lantern in his hand, he
    goes from house to house, looking at the doors.*)

Scene VIII

Cyrano, Christian, a Capuchin.

CYRANO

(*To the* CAPUCHIN)
What are you doing? Renewing Diogenes's search?

THE CAPUCHIN
I'm looking for the house of Madame . . .

CHRISTIAN

What a nuisance!

THE CAPUCHIN

Magdeleine Robin.

CHRISTIAN

What does he want?

CYRANO

(*To the* CAPUCHIN, *showing him an uphill street*)
It's that way. Straight ahead.

THE CAPUCHIN
Thank you. I'll say all the prayers in my rosary for you.
    (*He leaves.*)

CYRANO
Good luck! May my best wishes go with you!
    (*Returns to* CHRISTIAN.)

Scene IX

Cyrano, Christian.

CHRISTIAN
You must get that kiss for me!

CYRANO
No!

CHRISTIAN
Sooner or later ...

CYRANO
Yes, it's true. Sooner or later there will be an ecstatic moment when your mouths are drawn together, because of your blond mustache and her pink lips! (*To himself*) I prefer it to be because of ...
(*Sound of the window being opened again.* CHRISTIAN *hides under the balcony.*)

Scene X

Cyrano, Christian, Roxane.

ROXANE
(*Coming out onto the balcony*)
Are you still there? We were talking about ... about a ...

CYRANO
A kiss. The word is so sweet! Why should you be afraid to say it? If even the word burns your lips, what will the act do? Don't be alarmed; you've already given up your bantering tone and gradually drifted from smiles to sighs, and then from sighs to tears! Let yourself drift a little further: you'll cross the distance from tears to a kiss in the time it takes for one quiver of joy!

ROXANE
Stop!

CYRANO
After all, what is a kiss? A vow made at closer range, a more precise promise, a confession that contains its own proof, a seal placed on a pact that has already been signed;

125

it's a secret told to the mouth rather than to the ear, a fleeting moment filled with the hush of eternity, a communion that has the fragrance of a flower, a way of living by the beat of another heart, and tasting another soul on one's lips!

ROXANE

Stop!

CYRANO

Kisses are so noble that the Queen of France once gave one to an English lord!

ROXANE

But I don't see . . .

CYRANO
(*Becoming more impassioned*)
Like the Duke of Buckingham, I've suffered in silence; like him, I worship a queen;* like him, I'm sad and faithful. . . .

ROXANE

And like him, you're handsome!

CYRANO
(*Aside, abruptly sobered*)
Ah, yes, I'm handsome; I was forgetting that. . . .

ROXANE

Come to me! Come and give me that matchless flower . . .

CYRANO
(*Pushing* CHRISTIAN *toward the balcony*)
Climb up to her!

ROXANE

. . . that communion . . .

CYRANO

Climb!

ROXANE

. . . that hush of eternity . . .

CYRANO

Climb!

* George Villiers, Duke of Buckingham (1592–1629) was in love with the Queen of France, Anne of Austria (1601–1666), wife of Louis XIII. Alexandre Dumas wrote a fictionalized version of their romance in *The Three Musketeers.*

CHRISTIAN

(*Hesitating*)
But now it seems to me that it's wrong!

ROXANE

... that taste of another soul!

CYRANO

(*Pushing him*)
Climb, you fool!
(CHRISTIAN *stands on the bench, then climbs up onto the balcony.*)

CHRISTIAN

Ah, Roxane!
(*Takes her in his arms and kisses her.*)

CYRANO

What a strange pang in my heart! I'm like Lazarus at the feast—a feast of love! I must content myself with very little, but I still have a few small crumbs. Yes, I feel something of that kiss in my heart, because Roxane is kissing not only Christian's lips, but also the words I spoke to her! (*The lutes begin playing again.*) A sad tune and a happy one: the Capuchin! (*Takes a few rapid steps, pretending to have just arrived, and calls out loudly.*) Roxane!

ROXANE

Who is it?

CYRANO

It's I. I was passing by. . . . Is Christian still here?

CHRISTIAN

(*Surprised*)
Cyrano!

ROXANE

Good evening, cousin.

CYRANO

Good evening, cousin.

ROXANE

I'm coming down!
(*She disappears into the house. The* CAPUCHIN *enters in the background.*)

CHRISTIAN

(*Seeing him*)
No! Not again!
(*Follows* ROXANE.)

Scene XI

Cyrano, Christian, Roxane, the Capuchin, Ragueneau.

THE CAPUCHIN

This is Magdeleine Robin's house!

CYRANO

You said "Rolin" before.

THE CAPUCHIN

No, I said "Robin!" R-O-B-I-N!

ROXANE

(Appearing in the doorway of the house, followed by RAGUENEAU, *who carries a lantern, and* CHRISTIAN)
Who's this?

THE CAPUCHIN

I have a letter for you.

CHRISTIAN

A letter?

THE CAPUCHIN

(To ROXANE)
It surely concerns some holy matter. It's from a worthy lord who . . .

ROXANE

(To CHRISTIAN)
It's from De Guiche!

CHRISTIAN

How dare he . . .

ROXANE

He won't bother me much longer! *(Opening the letter)* I love you, and if . . . *(By the light of* RAGUENEAU'*s lantern, she reads the letter to herself in a low voice.)* "The drums are beating and my regiment is preparing to leave. Everyone believes that I have already gone, but I am staying, in disobedience to your orders. I am in a monastery. This letter is to inform you that I will soon come to visit you. The monk who will deliver it to you is as simpleminded as a goat, so there is no danger of his guessing my plan. Your lips have smiled at me too much today; I must see them again. I hope that you have already forgiven my boldness, and I remain your . . ." And so on. *(To the* CAPUCHIN) Father, you must hear what's in this letter. Listen. *(The others gather around her and she pretends to read aloud.)*

"You must bow to the Cardinal's will, however difficult it may be for you. This letter will be delivered into your charming hands by a saintly, intelligent, and discreet Capuchin. You will inform him that we wish him to give you the blessing of holy matrimony . . ." (*Turns the page.*) ". . . in your house, and without delay. Christian must secretly become your husband. I have already sent him to you. I know that you dislike him, but you must accept the Cardinal's decision, and you may rest assured that heaven will bless you for your resignation. With the respect that I have always borne for you, I remain your humble and devoted . . ." And so on.

THE CAPUCHIN

(*Beaming*)
I told you it was from a very worthy lord! I knew it could only concern some holy matter!

ROXANE

(*To* CHRISTIAN, *in an undertone*)
I read letters well, don't I?

CHRISTIAN

Hm!

ROXANE

(*Loudly, with despair*)
Oh! This is horrible!

THE CAPUCHIN

(*Turning the light of his lantern on* CYRANO)
Are you the . . .

CHRISTIAN

No, *I* am!

THE CAPUCHIN

(*Turns the light on* CHRISTIAN, *then, seeing how handsome he is, appears to become suspicious.*)
But . . .

ROXANE

(*Quickly, pretending to read again*)
"P.S. You will make a gift of a thousand francs to the monastery."

THE CAPUCHIN

A worthy, worthy lord! (*To* ROXANE) Resign yourself!

ROXANE

(*In a tone of martyrdom*)
I am resigned. (*While* RAGUENEAU *opens the door for the*

CAPUCHIN, *whom* CHRISTIAN *has invited to enter, she speaks softly to* CYRANO.) De Guiche will soon be here. Delay him, don't let him come in until . . .

CYRANO

I understand. (*To the* CAPUCHIN) How long will you need for the wedding ceremony?

THE CAPUCHIN

About a quarter of an hour.

CYRANO
   (*Pushing them all toward the house*)
Hurry! I'll stay here.

ROXANE

   (*To* CHRISTIAN)
Come!
   (*They go inside.*)

Scene XII

Cyrano, alone.

CYRANO

How can I make De Guiche waste a quarter of an hour? (*Leaps onto the bench and climbs up the wall, toward the balcony.*) Up we go! . . . I have my plan! (*The lutes begin playing a mournful melody.*) Aha! A man is coming! (*The tremolo becomes sinister.*) No doubt of it this time! (*He is now on the balcony. He pushes his hat down over his eyes, takes off his sword, wraps his cloak around himself, leans forward, and looks down.*) No, it's not too high. . . . (*He sits on the railing, takes one of the long tree branches that overhang the garden wall, pulls it toward him, and holds it with both hands, ready to swing down.*) I'm going to trouble this peaceful atmosphere a little!

Scene XIII

Cyrano, De Guiche.

DE GUICHE
   (*Entering masked, groping in the darkness*)
What's happened to that cursed Capuchin?

CYRANO

My voice! What if he recognizes it? (*Lets go of the branch with one hand and makes the motion of turning an invisible key.*) There! I've unlocked my Gascon accent!

DE GUICHE

(*Looking at the house*)
Yes, this is it. I can hardly see where I'm going. This mask is so annoying! (*He walks toward the door.* CYRANO *leaps from the balcony, holding the branch, which bends and sets him down between* DE GUICHE *and the door. He pretends to fall heavily, as if from a great height, and lies motionless on the ground, as though dazed.* DE GUICHE *jumps back.*) What! . . . What's this? . . . (*He looks up, but the branch has already sprung back into place. Seeing nothing but the sky, he is mystified.*) Where did this man fall from?

CYRANO

(*Sitting up, and speaking with a Gascon accent*)
From the moon!

DE GUICHE

Did you say . . .

CYRANO

(*Dreamily*)
What time is it?

DE GUICHE

He's lost his reason!

CYRANO

What time is it? What country is this? What day? What season?

DE GUICHE

But . . .

CYRANO

I'm still dazed.

DE GUICHE

Sir . . .

CYRANO

I fell from the moon like a cannonball!

DE GUICHE

(*Impatiently*)
Look, sir . . .

CYRANO

(*Loudly and emphatically, standing up*)
I fell from the moon!

DE GUICHE

(*Stepping back*)
Very well, then, you fell from the moon! (*Aside*) He may
be a maniac!

CYRANO

(*Advancing toward him*)
And I don't mean it metaphorically!

DE GUICHE

But ...

CYRANO

A hundred years ago, or perhaps a minute ago—I have no
idea how long my fall lasted—I was on that yellow sphere!

DE GUICHE

(*Shrugging*)
Yes, of course. Let me pass.

CYRANO

(*Stepping in front of him*)
Where am I? Be frank, don't hide anything from me! What
is this place where I've just fallen like a meteorite?

DE GUICHE

Enough of this!

CYRANO

As I was falling, I wasn't able to choose my destination,
and I don't know where I've landed. Has the weight of my
posterior brought me back to earth, or to another moon?

DE GUICHE

Sir, I ...

CYRANO

(*With a cry of terror that makes* DE GUICHE *step back
again*)
Oh! My God! I see I've fallen into a country where people
have black faces!

DE GUICHE

(*Putting his hand to his face*)
What ...

CYRANO

(*With a great show of fear*)
Am I in Algiers? Are you a native?

DE GUICHE
(*Who has felt his mask*)
I'm wearing a mask.

CYRANO
(*Pretending to be somewhat reassured*)
Then am I in Venice, or Genoa?

DE GUICHE
(*Trying to get past him*)
A lady is expecting me. . . .

CYRANO
Ah, then I'm in Paris!

DE GUICHE
(*Smiling in spite of himself*)
This lunatic is rather amusing!

CYRANO
You're smiling?

DE GUICHE
Yes, but I still want you to let me pass!

CYRANO
(*Beaming*)
I've fallen back into Paris! (*Thoroughly at ease, smiling,
brushing himself off, bowing*) Excuse me; I've just come
by the latest whirlwind and I have ether all over me. Such
a journey! My eyes are full of stardust. I still have a little
planet fur on my spurs. (*Picks something off his sleeve.*)
A comet hair on my doublet! (*Pretends to blow it away.*)

DE GUICHE
(*Beside himself with exasperation*)
Sir! . . .
(*Just as* DE GUICHE *is about to pass,* CYRANO *stops him
by putting out his leg, as though to show him something
on it.*)

CYRANO
The Great Bear bit me as I passed. Look, you can see the
tooth marks on my leg. Then, when I swerved to avoid
Orion's Sword, I fell into the Scales. The pointer still marks
my weight. (*Quickly prevents* DE GUICHE *from passing and
takes hold of his doublet.*) If you were to squeeze my nose,
sir, milk would spurt from it.

DE GUICHE
Milk?

CYRANO

From the Milky Way!

DE GUICHE

Oh! Stop this nonsense and let me . . .

CYRANO

Not yet. I haven't finished my story. (*Folds his arms.*)
Would you believe me if I told you that during my fall I
discovered that Sirius wears a nightcap? (*In a confidential
tone*) The Little Bear is still too small to bite! (*Laughs.*)
When I went through the Lyre, I broke one of its strings!
(*Proudly*) But I intend to write a book* about all that.
When I publish it, I'll take the stars I brought back in my
cloak, at the risk of burning it, and use them for asterisks!

DE GUICHE

Sir, I've been very patient with you. Now will you please . . .

CYRANO

I understand. I'll be glad to oblige you.

DE GUICHE

At last!

CYRANO

You want me to tell you what the moon is like and whether
anyone lives there, isn't that right?

DE GUICHE

No! No! I want to . . .

CYRANO

Yes, of course—you want to know how I got to the moon.
I did it by a method that I invented myself.

DE GUICHE

(*Discouraged*)
He's raving mad!

CYRANO

(*Disdainfully*)
I didn't simply make a new version of Regiomontanus's†
stupid eagle or Archytas's timid dove.

---

* The real Cyrano de Bergerac wrote a book describing a journey
to the moon: *Histoire comique des Etats et Empires de la Lune.*

† Regiomontanus (1436–1476, real name Johann Müller), German
mathematician and astronomer who is said to have made a mechanical bird capable of flying.

DE GUICHE

He's a madman, but a learned madman.

CYRANO

No, I didn't imitate anything that had been done before!
(DE GUICHE *succeeds in getting past him. He walks toward*
ROXANE'S *door while* CYRANO *follows him, ready to take
hold of him.*) I invented six ways to violate the virgin sky!

DE GUICHE

(*Stopping and turning around*)
Six?

CYRANO

(*Volubly*)
I could have clothed my naked body with crystal bottles
full of dew and exposed myself to the morning sun; then,
as the sun drew up the dew, I would have been drawn up
with it!

DE GUICHE

(*Surprised, and taking a step toward* CYRANO)
Yes, that's one way!

CYRANO

(*Stepping back to lead him away from the door*)
And I could have rarefied the air in a cedar chest by means
of twenty burning-mirrors* suitably arranged, thus producing a great rush of wind that would have sent me on my
way!

DE GUICHE

(*Taking another step toward him*)
Two!

CYRANO

(*Still moving back*)
Or, with my mechanical skill and my knowledge of pyro-
technics, I could have constructed a large steel grasshopper
propelled by successive explosions of gunpowder, and rid-
den it into the blue realm of the stars!

DE GUICHE

(*Following him without realizing it, and counting on his
fingers*)
Three!

---

* A burning-mirror is a concave mirror used for producing intense
heat by concentrating the sun's rays.

CYRANO

Since smoke tends to rise, I could have blown enough of it into a globe to carry me away!

DE GUICHE

(*Increasingly surprised, and still following him*)
Four!

CYRANO

Since the new moon likes to suck up the marrow of cattle, I could have coated my body with it!

DE GUICHE

(*Fascinated*)
Five!

CYRANO

(*Who, while speaking, has led him to the other side of the square, near a bench*)
Finally, I could have sat on a sheet of iron and thrown a magnet into the air. It's a very good method: the iron follows the magnet in its flight, then you quickly throw the magnet again, and keep repeating the process until you've reached the moon!

DE GUICHE

Six! . . . But which of those six excellent methods did you choose?

CYRANO

A seventh!

DE GUICHE

Amazing! Tell me about it.

CYRANO

Try to guess.

DE GUICHE

This rascal is becoming interesting!

CYRANO

(*Making a sound of waves, with broad, mysterious gestures*)
Hoo! . . . Hoo! . . .

DE GUICHE

What's that?

CYRANO

Can't you guess?

DE GUICHE

No!

CYRANO

The tide! . . . After taking a dip in the sea, I lay on the beach at the hour when the moon was exerting the pull that causes the tides, and I was lifted into the air—headfirst, of course, since it was my hair that held the most moisture. I was rising straight up, slowly and effortlessly, like an angel, when suddenly I felt a shock! Then . . .

DE GUICHE

(*Sitting down on the bench, seized with curiosity*)
Yes? Then what?

CYRANO

Then . . . (*Resumes his natural voice.*) The quarter of an hour has passed, so I won't keep you any longer. The wedding is over.

DE GUICHE

(*Leaping to his feet*)
I must be losing my mind! That voice! . . . (*The door of the house opens.* LACKEYS *appear, carrying lighted candelabra. The stage lighting becomes brighter.* CYRANO *takes off his hat, whose brim has remained turned down throughout the scene.*) And that nose! . . . Cyrano!

CYRANO

(*Bowing*)
At your service. They've just been married.

DE GUICHE

Who? (*He turns around. Tableau. Behind thé* LACKEYS, ROXANE *and* CHRISTIAN *are holding hands. The* CAPUCHIN *follows them, smiling.* RAGUENEAU *is also holding a candelabrum. The* DUENNA *brings up the rear, looking bewildered and wearing a dressing gown.*) Good God!

Scene XIV

Cyrano, De Guiche, Roxane, Christian, the Capuchin, Ragueneau, Lackeys, the Duenna.

DE GUICHE

(*To* ROXANE)
You! (*With amazement, recognizing* CHRISTIAN) And he?

. . . (*Bowing to* ROXANE *with admiration*) I congratulate you on your cleverness! (*To* CYRANO) And to you, the great inventor, my compliments! Your story would have stopped a saint at the gates of heaven! Write down the details of it, because you really could use them in a book!

CYRANO
(*Bowing*)
I promise to follow your advice.

THE CAPUCHIN
(*Showing the two lovers to* DE GUICHE *and nodding his white-bearded head with satisfaction*)
Here's the handsome couple you've united, my son!

DE GUICHE
(*Giving him an icy look*)
Yes. (*To* ROXANE) And now you must tell your husband good-by, madame.

ROXANE
Why?

DE GUICHE
(*To* CHRISTIAN)
The regiment is about to leave. Join it!

ROXANE
To go to war?

DE GUICHE
Of course!

ROXANE
But the Cadets aren't going!

DE GUICHE
Yes, they are. (*Takes the envelope from his pocket.*) Here's the order. (*To* CHRISTIAN) Deliver it at once, Baron.

ROXANE
(*Throwing herself in* CHRISTIAN'*s arms*)
Christian!

DE GUICHE
(*Sneering, to* CYRANO)
The wedding night is still a long way off!

CYRANO
(*Aside*)
He thinks that's bitter news to me!

CHRISTIAN

(*To* ROXANE)
Oh! Kiss me again!

CYRANO

Come, come, enough!

CHRISTIAN

(*Continuing to kiss* ROXANE)
It's hard to leave her.... You can't know....

CYRANO

(*Trying to lead him away*)
I do know....
    (*Drums are heard beating in the distance.*)

DE GUICHE

(*Who has gone upstage*)
The regiment! It's leaving!

ROXANE

(*To* CYRANO, *clutching* CHRISTIAN, *whom he is still trying to lead away*)
I trust you to look after him! Promise me that nothing will endanger his life!

CYRANO

I'll do my best, but I can't promise anything.

ROXANE

(*Still holding* CHRISTIAN *back*)
Promise me that you'll make him be very careful!

CYRANO

I'll try, but ...

ROXANE

(*Still holding* CHRISTIAN)
Promise me that he'll never be cold during that terrible siege!

CYRANO

I'll do whatever I can, but ...

ROXANE

(*Still holding* CHRISTIAN)
Promise me that he'll be faithful!

CYRANO

Of course he will! But ...

ROXANE

(*Still holding* CHRISTIAN)
Promise me that he'll write often!

CYRANO

(*Stopping*)
Ah! That's one thing I can promise you!

CURTAIN

ACT FOUR

The Gascon Cadets

The post occupied by CARBON DE CASTEL-JALOUX's *company in the siege of Arras.*

In the background, an embankment crossing the entire stage. Beyond, a plain covered with siegeworks. Far off in the distance, the walls and rooftops of Arras are silhouetted against the sky.

Tents, scattered weapons, drums, etc. Daybreak is near. Yellowish glow in the east. Sentries at intervals. Campfires.

Wrapped in their cloaks, the GASCON CADETS *are asleep.* CARBON *and* LE BRET *are awake. They are both pale and gaunt.* CHRISTIAN, *sleeping like the others, is in the foreground, with the light of a campfire on his face. Silence.*

Scene I

Christian, Carbon de Castel-Jaloux, Le Bret, the Cadets, then Cyrano.

LE BRET

It's horrible!

CARBON

Yes. Not one scrap of food left.

LE BRET

Mordious!

CARBON

(*Motioning him to speak more softly*)
Do your swearing in a whisper! You'll wake them up! (*To the* CADETS) Sh! Sleep! (*To* LE BRET) As the proverb says, he who sleeps dines.

LE BRET

Yes, but that's not much comfort when you have insomnia! What a famine!
(*A few shots are heard in the distance.*)

CARBON

Damn those shots! They'll wake my children! (*To the* CADETS, *who have begun to raise their heads*) Go back to sleep!
(*The* CADETS *settle down again, then there are more shots, from closer range.*)

A CADET

(*Stirring*)
What, again?

CARBON

It's nothing, only Cyrano coming back.
(*The heads that have been raised are lowered again.*)

A SENTRY

(*Offstage*)
Halt! Who goes there?

CYRANO'S VOICE

Bergerac!

THE SENTRY ON THE PARAPET

Halt! Who goes there?

CYRANO

(*Appearing on the parapet*)
Bergerac, you idiot!
(*Comes down from the parapet.* LE BRET *anxiously goes forward to meet him.*)

LE BRET

Thank God you're back!

CYRANO

(*Motioning him not to awaken anyone*)
Sh!

LE BRET

Are you wounded?

CYRANO

You know very well that they make it a habit to miss me
every morning!

LE BRET

Don't you think it's going a little too far to risk your life
every day to send a letter?

CYRANO

(*Stopping in front of* CHRISTIAN)
I promised he would write often! (*Looks at him.*) He's
asleep. His face is pale. If poor Roxane knew he was dying
of hunger . . . But he's still handsome!

LE BRET

Hurry, go and get some sleep!

CYRANO

Don't nag me, Le Bret! And don't worry: I always cross
the Spanish lines at a place where I know the soldiers get
drunk every night.

LE BRET

You ought to bring us some food.

CYRANO

I have to travel light to get through! . . . But you can expect a change by this evening. If I saw what I think I saw,
the French will soon either eat or die.

LE BRET

Tell me about it!

CYRANO

No, I'm not sure. . . . You'll see!

CARBON

We're the besiegers, and yet we're starving! It's shameful!

LE BRET

Unfortunately, nothing could be more complicated than
this siege. We're besieging Arras, we ourselves are caught
in a trap, the Cardinal Prince of Spain is besieging us. . . .

CYRANO

Someone ought to come and besiege *him*.

LE BRET

Excuse me if I don't laugh.

CYRANO

You're excused.

LE BRET

To think that every day you risk a life like yours to carry ... (*Sees* CYRANO *walking toward a tent.*) Where are you going?

CYRANO

I'm going to write another one.
(*Lifts the flap of the tent and disappears.*)

Scene II

The same, without Cyrano.

(*Daylight is advancing; the pink glow of dawn has appeared. The town of Arras is illuminated on the horizon. From the left, a distant cannon shot is heard, immediately followed by a drumbeat. Other drums begin beating, nearer. The drumbeats answer each other, draw closer, are heard almost on the stage, and finally fade away to the right, crossing the camp. Sounds of awakening. Officers' voices in the distance.*)

CARBON

(*With a sigh*)
Reveille, alas! (*The* CADETS *stir in their cloaks and stretch.*) Their delicious sleep has ended, and I know only too well what their first words will be!

A CADET

(*Sitting up*)
I'm hungry!

ANOTHER

I'm starving!

ALL

Oh! ...

CARBON

On your feet, all of you!

THIRD CADET

I can't stand up!

FOURTH CADET

I can't move!

FIRST CADET

(*Looking at himself in a piece of polished armor*)
My tongue is yellow—living on air has given me indigestion!

FIFTH CADET

I'd give my baron's coronet for a bite of cheese!

SIXTH CADET

If I don't get something to keep the walls of my stomach from growing together, I'll withdraw to my tent, like Achilles!

SEVENTH CADET

Yes! We must have food!

CARBON

(*Calling softly into the tent where* CYRANO *has gone*)
Cyrano!

OTHER CADETS

We're dying!

CARBON

(*Still softly, standing at the doorway of the tent*)
I need your help! You always know how to answer them—come and cheer them up!

SECOND CADET

(*Hurrying to the* FIRST CADET, *who is chewing something*)
What are you eating?

FIRST CADET

Ammunition wadding cooked in axle grease, using a steel helmet as a pot. There's not much game in this country!

ANOTHER CADET

(*Entering*)
I've just been hunting!

ANOTHER

(*Entering*)
I've been fishing in the river!

ALL

(*Standing up and rushing toward the two newcomers*)
What?—What have you brought?—A pheasant?—A carp?
—Show us!

THE FISHERMAN

A gudgeon!

THE HUNTER

A sparrow!

ALL

(*Exasperated*)
Enough!—Let's mutiny!

CARBON

Cyrano! Help!
(*It is now broad daylight.*)

Scene III

The same, with Cyrano.

CYRANO
(*Calmly coming out of the tent with a quill pen behind his ear and a book in his hand*)
What's the trouble? (*Silence. He speaks to the* FIRST CADET.) Why are you standing so stiffly?

FIRST CADET

I have to.

CYRANO

Why?

FIRST CADET

My stomach is so empty that if I bend at the waist I'll break in half!

CYRANO

Be glad you've lost weight: it may save your life.

FIRST CADET

How?

CYRANO

By making you a smaller target for the enemy!

SECOND CADET

I'm so hungry I could eat a whole side of beef!

CYRANO

Now there's a meaty remark!

THIRD CADET

My belly is hollow!

CYRANO

We'll use it for a drum.

FOURTH CADET

You must be as hungry as we are. How do you stand it?

CYRANO

I think of how long it's been since the last time I ate, and that makes me so sad I lose my appetite.

FIFTH CADET

I don't think about my last meal, I worry about my next one!

CYRANO

That's good. Maybe you'll worry yourself into a stew.

SIXTH CADET

There's nothing to relieve our hunger, nothing!

CYRANO

(*Tossing him the book he has been holding in his hand*)
Here, read the *Iliad:* it will give you food for thought.

SEVENTH CADET

In Paris, Cardinal Richelieu eats his fill!

CYRANO

Do you think he ought to send you a partridge?

SEVENTH CADET

Why not? And some wine to go with it!

CYRANO

I'll have Burgundy, please.

SEVENTH CADET

I'm sure Richelieu will be glad to send you some from his own cellar.

CYRANO

Of course—generosity is one of his cardinal virtues.

EIGHTH CADET

Why is it that *you* never complain about your hunger?

CYRANO

Because there's one thing I'm not hungry enough to swallow: my pride.

FIRST CADET

(*Shrugging*)
You're never at a loss for a clever remark.

CYRANO

Yes, and I hope that when death comes to me it will find me
fighting in a good cause and making a clever remark! I want
to be struck down by the only noble weapon, the sword,
wielded by an adversary worthy of me, and to die not in a
sickbed but on the field of glory, with sharp steel in my
heart and a flash of wit on my lips!

ALL THE CADETS

(*Shouting*)
I'm hungry!

CYRANO

(*Folding his arms*)
Can't you think of anything but food? . . . Come here,
Bertrandou. You're a fifer now, but you were once a
shepherd; take out your fife and play some of the old Gascon music for these gluttons! Let them hear those soft,
haunting melodies in which each note is like a little sister,
melodies that hold the sound of loved voices and have the
slowness of smoke rising from the chimneys of our home
villages, melodies that speak to us in our mother tongue!
(BERTRANDOU, *the old fifer, sits down and prepares his
fife.*) Your fife is now a sorrowful warrior, but while your
fingers move over it like birds dancing a minuet, let it
remember that before it was made of ebony it was a simple
reed! Let it marvel at its own song and recognize in it the
soul of its rustic, peaceful youth! (BERTRANDOU *begins playing melodies from the south of France.*) Listen, Gascons.
. . . He's no longer playing the martial fife: it's now the
flute of our forests! It's not a call to battle, but the slow
piping of our goatherds! Listen. . . . It's our valleys, our
moors, our woodlands; it's a dark-haired little cowherd
wearing a red beret; it's the sweetness of evenings on the
banks of the Dordogne. . . . Listen, Gascons: it's all of
Gascony!
   (*The* CADETS *have all sat down and dreamily bowed their
   heads. Now and then one of them furtively wipes away
   a tear with his sleeve or his cloak.*)

CARBON

(*Softly, to* CYRANO)
You're making them weep!

CYRANO

Yes, from homesickness! It's a nobler pain than hunger.
I'm glad that their suffering has shifted from their bellies to
their hearts.

CARBON

You'll weaken them by stirring up such feelings!

CYRANO

(*Motioning the drummer to approach*)
Not at all! The courage in their blood is easily awakened.
It takes only . . .
(*He makes a gesture and the drummer beats a roll.*)

ALL THE CADETS

(*Leaping to their feet and rushing for their weapons*)
What?—Where?—What is it?

CYRANO

(*Smiling*)
You see? It takes only a drumbeat! Farewell dreams, regrets, homesickness, memories of love! What the fife
brought, the drum has taken away!

A CADET

(*Looking upstage*)
Oh! Here comes Monsieur de Guiche!
(*The* CADETS *all murmur irritably.*)

CYRANO

(*Smiling*)
That's a flattering greeting!

THE CADET

He annoys us!

SECOND CADET

He's coming to strut in front of us with his big lace collar
over his armor!

THIRD CADET

A soldier shouldn't wear cloth over steel!

FIRST CADET

Not unless he has a boil on his neck!

SECOND CADET

He's not a soldier, he's a courtier!

FOURTH CADET

He's his uncle's nephew!

CARBON

He's still a Gascon.

FIRST CADET

Not a real one! A real Gascon is mad, and he's not. Don't
trust him, because there's nothing more dangerous than a
sane Gascon!

LE BRET
He looks pale.

FIFTH CADET

He's hungry, like the rest of us poor devils, but since his armor has gilded studs, his stomach cramps glitter in the sunlight!

CYRANO

(*Urgently*)

We mustn't let him see us looking miserable! Take out your cards, your pipes, your dice. . . . (*They all quickly begin playing cards and dice on drums, stools, and their cloaks spread out on the ground, and they light their long pipes.*) As for me, I'm going to read Descartes.

(*He walks slowly back and forth, reading from a small book that he has taken from his pocket. Tableau.* DE GUICHE *enters. The* CADETS *all seem happily absorbed in what they are doing.* DE GUICHE *is very pale. He walks toward* CARBON.)

Scene IV

The same, with De Guiche.

DE GUICHE

(*To* CARBON)

Ah! Good morning! (*Aside, with satisfaction, after they have observed each other a moment*) He looks green around the gills!

CARBON

(*Aside, also with satisfaction*)

His eyes are sunken, and big as saucers!

DE GUICHE

(*Looking at the* CADETS)

So here are the grumblers! . . . Yes, gentlemen, it's been reported to me from all sides that you jeer at me, that you mountain aristocrats, you country gentlemen, you rustic barons, have nothing but contempt for your colonel. You call me a schemer and a courtier, it upsets you to see a lace collar on my armor, and you're constantly expressing indignation at the idea that a man can be a Gascon without being a ragged pauper! (*Silence. The* CADETS *continue their games and smoking.*) Am I going to have you punished by your captain? No.

CARBON

Let me point out to you that I'm free to do as I see fit, and I don't choose to punish my men.

DE GUICHE

Oh?

CARBON

I've paid for my company; it's my own. I obey only battle orders.

DE GUICHE

That will do! (*To the* CADETS) I can afford to despise your mockery, because my conduct under fire is well known. Only yesterday, at Bapaume, I furiously drove back Count de Bucquoi. Bringing my men down upon his like an avalanche, I charged three times!

CYRANO

(*Without looking up from his book*)
And don't forget your white scarf.

DE GUICHE

(*Surprised and pleased*)
Ah, you know about that? . . . Yes, as I was rallying my men for the third charge, I was caught in a rush of fugitives and swept along toward the enemy. I was in danger of being captured or shot when I had the good sense to take off the scarf that showed my rank and drop it on the ground. I was thus able to slip away from the Spaniards without attracting attention, then come back to them, followed by all my men, and beat them! . . . Well, what do you think of that?
(*The* CADETS *do not seem to have been listening, but they now stop puffing on their pipes and suspend the movements of their card and dice games; they are waiting.*)

CYRANO

I think that Henry the Fourth would never have given up his white plume,* even when surrounded by the enemy.
(*Silent joy among the* CADETS. *They resume laying down their cards, rolling their dice, and smoking their pipes.*)

---

* Before the Battle of Ivry, in 1590, Henry IV said to his soldiers, "If you lose your banners, rally around my white plume; you will always find it on the path of honor and glory."

DE GUICHE

But my trick succeeded!
(*The* CADETS *again become motionless, waiting.*)

CYRANO

Perhaps, but I don't believe in declining the honor of being
a target. (*The* CADETS *resume their activities with growing
satisfaction.*) You and I, sir, have different ideas of courage. If I had been there when you dropped the scarf, I
would have picked it up and put it on.

DE GUICHE

That's nothing but Gascon bragging!

CYRANO

Bragging? Lend me the scarf and accept my offer to wear
it while I lead an assault today.

DE GUICHE

And that's a Gascon offer! You know very well that my
scarf remained on the riverbank, in a place that's now
under heavy enemy fire, so that no one can go and bring
it back.

CYRANO

(*Taking the white scarf from his pocket and holding it
out to* DE GUICHE)
Here it is.
(*Silence. The* CADETS *stifle their laughter behind their
cards and dice cups.* DE GUICHE *turns around and looks
at them. They immediately take on serious expressions
and resume their games. One of them casually whistles
a melody played earlier by the fifer.*)

DE GUICHE

(*Taking the scarf*)
Thank you. Now that I have this piece of white cloth, I
can use it for a signal that I was hesitating to make.
(*Climbs to the top of the embankment and waves the
scarf several times.*)

ALL THE CADETS

What! ...

THE SENTINEL ON THE PARAPET

I see a man down there, running away!

DE GUICHE

(*Returning*)
He's a false Spanish spy. He's very useful to me. He reports

to the enemy whatever I tell him, which makes it possible
for us to influence their decisions.

CYRANO

He's contemptible!

DE GUICHE

(*Nonchalantly tying his scarf around his neck*)
He's valuable. Now, what was I saying? . . . Ah, yes, I was
about to tell you some news. Last night, in a supreme effort
to get food for us, the Marshal quietly left for Dourlens,
where our supplies are. He'll arrive there by traveling across
the fields, but in order to come back safely he took so
many troops with him that we're now extremely vulnerable
to an enemy attack: half the army is absent!

CARBON

If the Spaniards knew that . . . But they don't, do they?

DE GUICHE

Yes, they know. And they're going to attack.

CARBON

Ah!

DE GUICHE

My false spy came to warn me. He said, "I can make the
attack come at any place you like, by reporting that it's
your most weakly defended point. Just tell me where." I
answered, "Very well, leave the camp and watch our lines.
I'll signal to you from the place I've chosen."

CARBON

(*To the* CADETS)
Gentlemen, prepare yourselves.
(*They all stand up. Sounds of swords and sword belts
being buckled on.*)

DE GUICHE

The attack will begin in an hour.

FIRST CADET

Oh. . . . In that case . . .
(*They all sit down again and resume their games.*)

DE GUICHE

(*To* CARBON)
The most important thing is to gain time. The Marshal will
soon be on his way back.

CARBON

And how shall we gain time?

DE GUICHE

You will be so kind as to fight till the last of you is killed.

CYRANO

Ah, so that's your revenge?

DE GUICHE

I won't pretend that if I liked you I would have chosen you and your men, but since you're known to be incomparably brave, I'm serving my king by serving my rancor.

CYRANO

(*Bowing*)

Allow me to be grateful to you, sir.

DE GUICHE

(*Returning his bow*)

I know that you like to fight against odds of a hundred to one. I'm sure this is an opportunity you wouldn't have wanted to miss.

(*Goes upstage with* CARBON)

CYRANO

(*To the* CADETS)

Gentlemen, your Gascon coat of arms bears six chevrons, blue and gold. We're about to add one more, of a different color: blood-red!

(DE GUICHE *is talking quietly with* CARBON *in the background. Orders are being given. Preparations to meet the attack are being made.* CYRANO *goes to* CHRISTIAN, *who is standing motionless, with his arms folded.*)

CYRANO

(*Putting his hand on* CHRISTIAN's *shoulder*)

Christian?

CHRISTIAN

(*Shaking his head*)

Roxane. . . .

CYRANO

Yes, I know. . . .

CHRISTIAN

I wish I could at least pour out my heart to her in one last letter.

CYRANO

I thought something might happen today, so . . . (*Takes a letter from his doublet.*) . . . I wrote your farewell.

CHRISTIAN

Let me see!

CYRANO

Do you want . . .

CHRISTIAN

(*Taking the letter*)
Of course! (*Opens it and begins reading it, then stops.*)
What's this?

CYRANO

Where?

CHRISTIAN

Here—this little stain.

CYRANO

(*Quickly takes the letter back and looks at it with an innocent expression.*)
A stain?

CHRISTIAN

It was made by a tear!

CYRANO

Yes. . . . A poet is sometimes caught up in his own game; that's what makes it so fascinating. This letter, you understand . . . It was so moving that I made myself weep while I was writing it.

CHRISTIAN

Weep?

CYRANO

Yes, because . . . Dying is no great matter. What's unbearable is the thought of never seeing her again. And it's true: I'll never see her . . . (CHRISTIAN *looks at him.*) . . . we'll never . . . (*Quickly*) . . . you'll never . . .

CHRISTIAN

(*Snatching the letter from him*)
Give me that letter!
(*A distant clamor is heard from the edge of the camp.*)

SENTRY'S VOICE

My God! Who can that be?
(*Shots, shouts, jingling of harness bells*)

CARBON

What is it?

THE SENTRY

(Now on the parapet)
A carriage!
(Everyone rushes to look.)

VOICES

What!—In the camp?—It's coming this way!—It seems to
have come from the direction of the enemy!—The enemy?
—Shoot!—No! Didn't you hear what the driver shouted?—
What was it?—He said, "King's service!"
*(Everyone is now on the parapet, looking down. The
sound of the jingling bells is coming closer.)*

DE GUICHE

King's service?
(The men all come down and fall into line.)

CARBON

Hats off, everyone!

DE GUICHE

(Shouting into the wings)
King's service! . . . Line up, you rabble! Don't you know
how to receive a carriage in the king's service?
*(The carriage enters at a rapid trot. It is covered with
mud and dust. The curtains are drawn. Two* FOOTMEN
behind. It stops abruptly.)

CARBON

(Shouting)
Beat the general salute!
(Ruffle of drums. All the CADETS *take off their hats.)*

DE GUICHE

Lower the step!
(Two men rush forward. The carriage door opens.)

ROXANE

(Alighting from the carriage)
Good morning!
*(The men have bowed low; hearing the sound of a
woman's voice, they all straighten up at once. Stupefac-
tion)*

Scene V

The same, with Roxane.

DE GUICHE

King's service? You?

ROXANE

I'm in the service of the greatest of all kings: love!

CYRANO

Oh! My God!

CHRISTIAN

(*Hurrying to her*)
You! Why?

ROXANE

This siege had lasted too long!

CHRISTIAN

Why . . .

ROXANE

I'll tell you!

CYRANO

(*Who, at the sound of her voice, has remained rooted to the spot, not daring to turn his eyes toward her*)
I can't look at her. . . .

DE GUICHE

You can't stay here!

ROXANE

(*Gaily*)
Yes I can! Would you please bring me a drum to sit on? (*Sits on the drum that is brought for her.*) Thank you! (*Laughs.*) They shot at my carriage! (*Proudly*) We met a patrol! . . . It looks as if it had been made from a pumpkin, like the carriage in the fairy tale, doesn't it? And my footmen look as if they had once been rats. (*Throws a kiss to* CHRISTIAN.) Good morning! (*Looks at everyone.*) You don't seem very cheerful! . . . Did you know that Arras is a long way from Paris? (*Notices* CYRANO.) Cousin! Delighted to see you!

CYRANO

(*Approaching*)
And I'm amazed! How . . .

ROXANE

How did I find the army? It was quite simple: I went where I saw that the countryside had been laid waste. Oh, such horrors! I would never have believed them if I hadn't seen them! Gentlemen, if that's how you serve your king, I much prefer to serve mine!

CYRANO

This is insane! How the devil did you get here?

ROXANE

I went through the Spanish lines.

FIRST CADET

Trust a woman to do a thing like that!

DE GUICHE

How were you able to pass?

LE BRET

It must have been very difficult!

ROXANE

Not very. I simply rolled along in my carriage. Whenever a Spanish officer gave me a suspicious look, I smiled at him sweetly from the window, and since, with all due deference to the French, Spaniards are the most gallant gentlemen in the world, I was always allowed to continue on my way.

CARBON

I'm sure your smile is a passport that would let you go anywhere! But you must have been asked to say where you were going.

ROXANE

Yes, often. I always answered, "I'm going to see my lover." No matter how fierce he had looked before, the Spanish officer would solemnly close the door of my carriage, and with a gesture that any king would have envied, wave away the muskets that had already been aimed at me. Then, superbly gracious and proud, with his spurs thrusting out beneath his lace and the plume of his hat floating in the breeze, he would bow and say, "Pass, Señorita!"

CHRISTIAN

But Roxane . . .

ROXANE

Yes, I said "my lover"—forgive me! But don't you understand that if I'd said "my husband," no one would have let me pass?

CHRISTIAN

But . . .

ROXANE

What's the matter?

DE GUICHE

You must leave here!

ROXANE

Leave?

CYRANO

Yes, and quickly!

LE BRET

Immediately!

CHRISTIAN

Yes!

ROXANE

But why?

CHRISTIAN

(*Embarrassed*)
Because . . .

CYRANO

(*Embarrassed*)
In three-quarters of an hour . . .

DE GUICHE

(*Embarrassed*)
Or maybe an hour . . .

CARBON

(*Embarrassed*)
You'd better . . .

LE BRET

(*Embarrassed*)
You might . . .

ROXANE

I'm staying. There's going to be a battle, isn't there?

ALL

Oh, no!

ROXANE

He's my husband! (*Throws herself into* CHRISTIAN'*s arms.*)
Let them kill me with you!

CHRISTIAN

Such a look in your eyes!

ROXANE

Do I have to tell you why?

DE GUICHE

(*Desperately*)
This is a terribly dangerous post!

ROXANE

(*Turning around*)
Dangerous?

CYRANO

He knows what he's saying: he gave it to us!

ROXANE

(*To* DE GUICHE)
Ah, so you wanted to make me a widow!

DE GUICHE

Oh! I swear to you that . . .

ROXANE

No! I don't care what happens to me now! I'm staying!
Besides, it's amusing.

CYRANO

What? You're both an intellectual and a heroine?

ROXANE

I'm your cousin, Monsieur de Bergerac.

A CADET

We'll defend you!

ROXANE

(*More and more excited*)
I believe it, my friends!

SECOND CADET

(*Ecstatically*)
The whole camp smells of iris!

ROXANE

And I'm wearing a hat that will look good in the battle! . . .
(*Looks at* DE GUICHE.) Don't you think it's time for you to
leave? The fighting may begin. . . .

DE GUICHE

This is too much! I'm going to inspect my cannons, and
then I'll come back. . . . You still have time: change your
mind!

ROXANE

Never!
(DE GUICHE *leaves.*)

Scene VI

The same, without De Guiche.

CHRISTIAN

(*Beseechingly*)
Roxane! . . .

ROXANE

No!

FIRST CADET

(*To the others*)
She's staying!

ALL

(*Jostling one another as they hurry to make themselves more presentable*)
A comb!—Soap!—Give me a needle, I have to sew up a hole!—A ribbon!—Your mirror!—My cuffs!—Your mustache curler!—A razor!

ROXANE

(*To* CYRANO, *who is again pleading with her*)
No! Nothing will make me leave this place!
(CARBON, *like the others, has tightened his buckles, dusted himself off, brushed his hat, straightened his plume, and put on his cuffs. He now approaches* ROXANE.)

CARBON

(*Ceremoniously, to* ROXANE)
That being the case, perhaps it would be fitting for me to introduce some of the gentlemen who will have the honor of dying before your eyes. (ROXANE *bows and waits, holding* CHRISTIAN'*s arm.* CARBON *begins making the introductions.*) Baron de Peyrescous de Colignac.

THE CADET

(*Bowing*)
Madame. . . .

CARBON

Baron de Casterac de Cahuzac . . . Vidame de Malgouyre Estressac Lésbas d'Escarabiot . . . Chevalier d'Antignac-Juzet . . . Baron Hillot de Blagnac-Saléchan de Castel-Crabioules . . .

ROXANE

Do you all have such long names?

BARON HILLOT

Yes, every one of us!

CARBON

(*To* ROXANE)
Open the hand that holds your handkerchief.

ROXANE

(*Opens her hand and the handkerchief falls.*)
Why?
(*The whole company makes a move to pick it up.*)

CARBON

(*Quickly picking it up*)
My company had no flag, but now it has the finest one in the whole army!

ROXANE

(*Smiling*)
It's rather small.

CARBON

(*Tying the handkerchief to his lance*)
But it's trimmed with lace!

A CADET

(*To the others*)
Now that I've seen her face, I could die without regret if I only had a little food in my stomach!

CARBON

(*Indignantly, having overheard*)
Shame! Speaking of food when an exquisite lady ...

ROXANE

But I'm hungry too! It must be the cool air. I'd like some pâté, cold chicken, and wine. Would you please bring it to me?
(*Consternation*)

A CADET

Bring it to you?

ANOTHER

Where the devil can we get it?

ROXANE

(*Calmly*)
In my carriage.

ALL

What!

ROXANE

But the food will have to be carved and served. Look at my coachman a little more closely, gentlemen, and you'll recognize a valuable man. If you like, each sauce will be reheated.

THE CADETS

(*Rushing toward the carriage*)
It's Ragueneau!
(*Loud cheers*)

ROXANE

(*Watching them*)
Poor men! . . .

CYRANO

(*Kissing her hand*)
You're our fairy godmother!

RAGUENEAU

(*Standing on the driver's seat like a mountebank in a public square*)
Gentlemen! . . .
(*Outburst of enthusiasm*)

THE CADETS

Bravo! Bravo!

RAGUENEAU

The Spaniards were so busy feasting their eyes that they didn't eye the feast!
(*Applause*)

CYRANO

(*Softly, to* CHRISTIAN)
Christian!

RAGUENEAU

Distracted by Beauty, they overlooked . . . (*Picks up a roast suckling pig on a tray and holds it aloft.*) . . . the Beast!
(*Applause. The tray is passed from hand to hand.*)

CYRANO

(*Softly, to* CHRISTIAN)
Please let me have a word with you.

RAGUENEAU

The sight they saw was so pleasant that they failed to notice . . . (*Picks up another tray.*) . . . this pheasant!
(*More enthusiasm. The tray is seized by a dozen eager hands.*)

CYRANO

(*Softly, to* CHRISTIAN)
I want to talk to you!

ROXANE

(*To the* CADETS *who are coming downstage, their arms laden with food*)
Set it down on the ground! (*Aided by the two imperturbable* FOOTMEN, *she begins making preparations for a picnic, then she speaks to* CHRISTIAN *just as* CYRANO *is about to take him aside.*) Come here and make yourself useful!
(CHRISTIAN *goes to help her.* CYRANO *shows signs of anxiety.*)

RAGUENEAU
A peacock with truffles!

FIRST CADET
(*Coming downstage with a blissful expression, carving himself a thick slice of ham*)
It will be easier to face death when we've stuffed our guts! (*Embarrassed, seeing* ROXANE) Excuse me, I mean when we've had a good meal.

RAGUENEAU
(*Throwing out the cushions of the carriage*)
The cushions are full of quail!
(*Tumult. The cushions are ripped open. Joyous laughter.*)

THIRD CADET
Hallelujah!

RAGUENEAU
(*Throwing out bottles*)
Wine! Ruby red and tawny white!

ROXANE
(*Tossing a folded tablecloth to* CYRANO)
Here, spread this tablecloth! It's time you did your share of the work!

RAGUENEAU
(*Brandishing a lantern that he has taken from the carriage*)
Each lantern is a little pantry!

CYRANO
(*Softly, to* CHRISTIAN, *while they spread the tablecloth together*)
I must talk to you before you talk to her!

RAGUENEAU
(*More and more exuberant*)
The handle of my whip is a sausage!

ROXANE
(*Pouring wine and handing out food*)
Since we're the ones who are going to be killed, we don't
care about the rest of the army! Everything for the Gascons! And if De Guiche comes, he's not invited! (*Going
from one to another*) There's plenty of time. . . . Don't
eat so fast! . . . Drink a little wine. . . . Why are you
weeping?

FIRST CADET
It's too good!

ROXANE
Sh! . . . Red or white? . . . Bring some bread for Monsieur
de Carbon! . . . A knife! . . . Hand me your plate. . . .
Would you like some of the crust? . . . I'll serve you! . . .
Burgundy? . . . A wing?

CYRANO
(*Following her, laden with dishes, helping her serve*)
She's adorable!

ROXANE
(*Going to* CHRISTIAN)
And what would *you* like?

CHRISTIAN
Nothing.

ROXANE
That won't do! At least take a biscuit dipped in muscatel.

CHRISTIAN
(*Trying to hold her back*)
Tell me why you came.

ROXANE
Later. For now, my time belongs to these poor men.

LE BRET
(*Who has gone upstage to pass a loaf of bread, at the
end of a lance, to the* SENTRY ON THE PARAPET)
Here comes De Guiche!

CYRANO
Quickly! Hide the food, the bottles, the baskets, everything!
And act as if nothing had happened! (*To* RAGUENEAU)
Hurry back to your driver's seat! . . . Is everything out of
sight?
(*In the twinkling of an eye, everything is hidden in the
tents or under cloaks and hats.* DE GUICHE *enters rap-
idly, then suddenly stops, sniffing. Silence.*)

Scene VII

The same, with De Guiche.

DE GUICHE
Something smells good here.

A CADET
(*Casually singing*)
Tra-la-la . . .

DE GUICHE
(*Looking at him*)
What's the matter with you? Your face is red.

THE CADET
It's nothing. We'll soon be fighting, and the thought of it
has made the blood rush to my head.

SECOND CADET
Poom-poom-poom . . .

DE GUICHE
(*Turning around*)
What's that?

SECOND CADET
(*Slightly drunk*)
Nothing. Just a song, a little song. . . .

DE GUICHE
You're in a gay mood!

SECOND CADET
It's because danger is approaching!

DE GUICHE
(*Calling* CARBON, *to give an order*)
Captain! I . . . (*Stops short when he sees him.*) You too!
You look happy as a lark!

CARBON
(*His face crimson, making an evasive gesture while hid-
ing a bottle of wine behind his back*)
Well, I . . .

DE GUICHE
I had one cannon left over. I had it brought there . . .
(*Points offstage.*) . . . in that corner. Your men can use it
if they need it.

A CADET

(*With affectation*)
How thoughtful of you!

SECOND CADET

(*Smiling graciously*)
We're deeply grateful for your concern!

DE GUICHE

You're both mad! . . . (*Curtly*) Since you're not used to
cannons, I must warn you not to stand behind this one
when it recoils.

FIRST CADET

Oh, pfft!

DE GUICHE

(*Going to him, furious*)
Look here! . . .

FIRST CADET

A Gascon's gun never moves to the rear!

DE GUICHE

(*Taking him by the arm and shaking him*)
You're drunk! . . . But on what?

FIRST CADET

(*Loftily*)
The smell of gunpowder!
(DE GUICHE *shrugs, pushes him away, and hurries to*
ROXANE.)

DE GUICHE

(*To* ROXANE)
Well, what have you decided?

ROXANE

I'm staying!

DE GUICHE

You must leave!

ROXANE

No!

DE GUICHE

In that case, I'll need a musket.

CARBON

What do you mean?

DE GUICHE

I'm staying too.

CYRANO

Sir, you've finally shown pure courage!

FIRST CADET

Are you really a Gascon, in spite of your lace?

ROXANE

What! . . .

DE GUICHE

I won't leave a woman in danger.

SECOND CADET
(*To the first*)
I think we can give him something to eat!
(*The food reappears as though by magic.*)

DE GUICHE
(*His face lighting up*)
Food!

THIRD CADET

It's coming out from under every cloak!

DE GUICHE
(*Haughtily, controlling himself*)
Do you think I'm going to eat your leavings?

CYRANO
(*Bowing*)
You're making progress!

DE GUICHE
(*Proudly*)
An empty belly won't stop me from fighting!

FIRST CADET
(*Enthusiastically*)
Spoken like a Gascon!

DE GUICHE
(*Laughing*)
I *am* a Gascon!

FIRST CADET
It's true! He's really one of us!
(*They all begin to dance.*)

CARBON
(*Reappearing on the parapet, after having disappeared behind the embankment a few moments earlier*)

I've stationed my pikemen. They're ready to fight to the
end!
(*Points to a row of pikes showing above the parapet.*)

DE GUICHE

(*To* ROXANE, *bowing*)
Will you accept my hand and go with me to inspect them?
(*She takes his hand and they go upstage toward the em-
bankment. The others follow them, taking off their hats.*)

CHRISTIAN

(*Hurrying to* CYRANO)
Tell me what you have to say, quickly!
(*As* ROXANE *appears on the parapet, the pikes disappear,
lowered in a salute, and a shout arises. She bows.*)

THE PIKEMEN

(*Offstage*)
Hurrah!

CHRISTIAN

What's your secret?

CYRANO

If Roxane should . . .

CHRISTIAN

Yes?

CYRANO

If she should speak to you about the letters . . .

CHRISTIAN

Go on!

CYRANO

Don't make the mistake of being surprised if . . .

CHRISTIAN

If what?

CYRANO

I must tell you! . . . It's quite simple. I thought of it as soon
as she arrived. You've . . .

CHRISTIAN

Tell me quickly!

CYRANO

You've . . . you've written to her more often than you think.

CHRISTIAN

I have?

CYRANO

Yes. I made myself the interpreter of your passion. I some-times wrote to her without telling you so.

CHRISTIAN

Oh?

CYRANO

It's quite simple!

CHRISTIAN

But we're blockaded! How did you send those letters?

CYRANO

I was able to get through the enemy lines before dawn.

CHRISTIAN

(*Folding his arms*)
And I suppose that was quite simple too? . . . How often have I been writing? Twice a week? Three times? Four?

CYRANO

More than that.

CHRISTIAN

Every day?

CYRANO

Yes, every day . . . twice.

CHRISTIAN

(*Violently*)
And you were carried away by the letters you wrote! So much so that you defied death . . .

CYRANO

(*Seeing* ROXANE *returning*)
Quiet! Not in front of her!
(*He quickly goes into his tent.*)

Scene VIII

Roxane, Christian; in the background, Cadets coming and going, with Carbon and De Guiche giving orders.

ROXANE

(*Hurrying to* CHRISTIAN)
And now, Christian! . . .

CHRISTIAN

(*Taking her hands*)

And now, Roxane, tell me why you traveled such appalling roads, infested with lawless soldiers, in order to join me here.

ROXANE

Because of your letters!

CHRISTIAN

What?

ROXANE

It's your fault if I'm in danger: your letters made me lose my reason! You've written so many of them in the last month, each more beautiful than the one before!

CHRISTIAN

Do you mean to say that because of a few love letters . . .

ROXANE

Yes! You can't know. . . . I've adored you since the evening when, under my window, you began to reveal your soul to me in a voice I'd never heard you use before, and when I read your letters it was like hearing that same voice. I could feel its tenderness enveloping me! Finally I had to come to you, no matter what the danger! Penelope wouldn't have calmly stayed home with her weaving if Ulysses had written to her as you've written to me! She would have become as ardent as Helen of Troy, thrown her work aside, and gone off to join him!

CHRISTIAN

But . . .

ROXANE

I read your letters over and over, until I began to feel faint! I knew I belonged to you totally! Each page was like a petal fallen from your soul. In every word I felt the flame of a powerful, sincere love. . . .

CHRISTIAN

Powerful and sincere? Did you really feel that in my letters, Roxane?

ROXANE

Oh, yes!

CHRISTIAN

And so you came. . . .

ROXANE

I had to. I'm yours, Christian, but I know you would lift me up if I tried to kneel before you, so I'm placing my soul at your feet, and it will always remain there! I've come to ask you to forgive me—and now is the time to ask forgiveness, since we may be about to die!—for having insulted you, in my frivolity, by first loving you only because you were handsome.

CHRISTIAN

(*In consternation*)
Oh, Roxane!

ROXANE

Later, when I became a little less frivolous, I was like a bird hopping before taking flight, held back by your handsome face and drawn forward by your soul. I then loved you for both of them together.

CHRISTIAN

And now?

ROXANE

Your true self has prevailed over your outer appearance. I now love you for your soul alone.

CHRISTIAN

(*Stepping back*)
Oh, Roxane!

ROXANE

I know how painful it is for a noble heart to be loved because of an accident of nature that will soon pass away. But you can be happy now: your thoughts outshine your face. Your handsomeness was what first attracted me, but now that my eyes are open I no longer see it!

CHRISTIAN

Oh! . . .

ROXANE

Do you still doubt your victory?

CHRISTIAN

(*Sorrowfully*)
Roxane . . .

ROXANE

I understand. You can't believe in that kind of love.

CHRISTIAN

I don't want it! I want to be loved simply for . . .

ROXANE

For what women have always loved in you till now? Let me love you in a better way!

CHRISTIAN

No! It was better before!

ROXANE

You don't know what you're saying! It's better now! I didn't really love you before. It's what makes you yourself that I now love. If you were less handsome . . .

CHRISTIAN

Enough!

ROXANE

I'd still love you. If you suddenly became ugly . . .

CHRISTIAN

Oh, don't say that!

ROXANE

I *will* say it!

CHRISTIAN

Even if I were ugly? . . .

ROXANE

Yes, even if you were ugly! I swear I'd still love you!

CHRISTIAN

My God!

ROXANE

Now are you happy?

CHRISTIAN

(*Choking*)
Yes. . . .

ROXANE

What's the matter?

CHRISTIAN

(*Gently pushing her away*)
Nothing. I must go and say a few words to someone. It will take only a minute.

ROXANE

But . . .

CHRISTIAN
(*Pointing to a group of* CADETS *in the background*)
My love has taken you away from those poor men. Go and
smile at them a little, since they're about to die.

ROXANE
(*Deeply moved*)
Dear Christian! . . .
(*She goes to the* CADETS, *who eagerly but respectfully
crowd around her.*)

Scene IX

*Christian, Cyrano; Roxane in the background, talking with
Carbon and some of the Cadets.*

CHRISTIAN
(*Calling outside* CYRANO's *tent*)
Cyrano?

CYRANO
(*Coming out of the tent, armed for battle*)
Yes? Oh! How pale you are!

CHRISTIAN
She doesn't love me anymore!

CYRANO
What!

CHRISTIAN
It's you she loves!

CYRANO
No!

CHRISTIAN
She loves only my soul now!

CYRANO
No!

CHRISTIAN
Yes! That means it's you she loves—and you love her too!

CYRANO
I?

CHRISTIAN

I know it's true.

CYRANO

Yes, it's true.

CHRISTIAN

You love her with all your heart.

CYRANO

More than that.

CHRISTIAN

Tell her so!

CYRANO

No!

CHRISTIAN

Why not?

CYRANO

Look at my face!

CHRISTIAN

She would still love me if I were ugly!

CYRANO

She told you that?

CHRISTIAN

Yes!

CYRANO

I'm glad she said it, but don't believe such nonsense! Yes, I'm very glad she had that thought. . . . But don't take her at her word! Don't become ugly—she would never forgive me!

CHRISTIAN

We'll see!

CYRANO

No, no!

CHRISTIAN

Let her choose! I want you to tell her everything!

CYRANO

No! I couldn't bear that torture!

CHRISTIAN

Do you expect me to kill your happiness because I'm handsome? That would be too unjust!

CYRANO

And do you expect me to kill yours because I happen to have been born with a gift for expressing . . . what you may feel?

CHRISTIAN

Tell her everything!

CYRANO

It's cruel of you to persist in tempting me!

CHRISTIAN

I'm tired of being my own rival!

CYRANO

Christian!

CHRISTIAN

Our wedding took place in secret, without witnesses. The marriage can be broken—if we survive!

CYRANO

You still persist! . . .

CHRISTIAN

I want to be loved for myself or not at all! We'll see what she decides. I'm going to walk to the end of the camp, then come back. Talk to her while I'm gone, and tell her she must choose one of us.

CYRANO

It will be you!

CHRISTIAN

I hope so! (*Calls.*) Roxane!

CYRANO

No! No!

ROXANE

(*Hurrying toward them*)
Yes?

CHRISTIAN

Cyrano has something important to tell you.
(*She expectantly turns to* CYRANO. CHRISTIAN *leaves.*)

Scene X

Roxane, Cyrano; then Le Bret, Carbon, the Cadets, Ragueneau, De Guiche, etc.

ROXANE

Something important?

CYRANO

(*Frantically*)
He's leaving! . . . (*To* ROXANE) No, it's really nothing. . . .
You must know how he is: he often sees importance where
none exists!

ROXANE

(*Anxiously*)
Does he doubt what I told him? Yes, he does! I could see he
doubted it!

CYRANO

(*Taking her hand*)
But was it really the truth?

ROXANE

Yes, I'd love him even if he were . . .
(*Hesitates.*)

CYRANO

(*Smiling sadly*)
The word embarrasses you in front of me?

ROXANE

No, I . . .

CYRANO

It won't hurt me! You'd love him even if he were ugly?

ROXANE

Yes! (*Several musket shots are heard offstage.*) The shoot-
ing seems to have begun.

CYRANO

(*Ardently*)
Even if he were hideous?

ROXANE

Yes!

CYRANO

Disfigured?

ROXANE

Yes!

CYRANO

Grotesque?

ROXANE

Nothing could make him seem grotesque to me!

CYRANO

You'd still love him?

ROXANE

Yes! Maybe even more!

CYRANO
(*Aside, losing his head*)
My God! Perhaps it's true! Can it be that happiness is here,
within my grasp? (*To* ROXANE) I . . . Roxane . . . Listen to
me. . . .

LE BRET
(*Entering rapidly and calling softly*)
Cyrano!

CYRANO
(*Turning around*)
Yes?

LE BRET

Sh!
(*Whispers something to* CYRANO, *who lets go of* ROXANE'S
hand with a cry.)

CYRANO

Oh!

ROXANE

What's the matter?

CYRANO
(*To himself, dazed*)
It's all over now.
(*More shots are heard.*)

ROXANE

What is it? Those shots . . .
(*Takes a few steps and looks offstage.*)

CYRANO

It's all over. Now I can never tell her!

ROXANE

What's happened?

CYRANO

(*Stopping her as she is about to rush forward*)
Nothing!
(*Some* CADETS *have entered, hiding the burden they are carrying. They group themselves to prevent* ROXANE *from approaching.*)

ROXANE

Those men . . .

CYRANO

(*Leading her away*)
Come away from them!

ROXANE

But what were you about to tell me?

CYRANO

Tell you? Oh, nothing. . . . Nothing, I swear! (*Solemnly*)
I swear that Christian's mind and soul were . . . (*Catches himself in alarm.*) . . . are the greatest . . .

ROXANE

Were?
(*She screams, runs to the group of* CADETS, *and pushes them aside.*)

CYRANO

It's all over.

ROXANE

(*Seeing* CHRISTIAN *lying wrapped in his cloak*)
Christian!

LE BRET

(*To* CYRANO)
The first shot fired by the enemy!
(ROXANE *throws herself onto* CHRISTIAN. *More shots. Clatter of weapons. Voices. Drumbeats.*)

CARBON

(*Holding his drawn sword*)
Here comes the attack! Get ready!
(*Followed by the* CADETS, *he climbs over the parapet.*)

ROXANE

Christian!

CARBON'S VOICE
(*From the other side of the embankment*)
Hurry!

ROXANE

Christian!

CARBON

Fall in!

ROXANE

Christian!

CARBON

Prepare your matches!*
(RAGUENEAU *hurries onstage, bringing water in a helmet.*)

CHRISTIAN
(*In a dying voice*)
Roxane . . .

CYRANO
(*Speaking rapidly and softly in* CHRISTIAN's *ear while* ROXANE, *distraught, tears a strip of cloth from her dress and dips it in the water to wash his wound*)
I told her everything. It's still you she loves!
(CHRISTIAN *closes his eyes.*)

ROXANE

Yes, my love?

CARBON

Take out your ramrods!

ROXANE
(*To* CYRANO)
He's not dead, is he?

CARBON

Bite open your charges!

ROXANE
I feel his cheek turning cold against mine!

CARBON

Ready! Aim!

* The match was the piece of burning cord used to set off the powder charge of a matchlock musket.

ROXANE

Here's a letter he was carrying! (*Opens it.*) For me!

CYRANO

(*Aside*)
My letter!

CARBON

Fire!
(*Shots, Cries. Sounds of battle.*)

CYRANO

(*Trying to draw his hand away from* ROXANE, *who
clutches it, kneeling*)
Roxane! The attack has begun!

ROXANE

(*Holding him back*)
Stay a little longer. He's dead. You were the only one who
knew him. (*She weeps gently.*) He was a great and won-
derful man, wasn't he?

CYRANO

(*Standing, bareheaded*)
Yes, Roxane.

ROXANE

A brilliant, captivating poet!

CYRANO

Yes, Roxane.

ROXANE

A magnificent mind!

CYRANO

Yes, Roxane.

ROXANE

A vast heart whose depths remained hidden from the world!
A noble and charming soul!

CYRANO

(*Firmly*)
Yes, Roxane!

ROXANE

(*Throwing herself onto* CHRISTIAN's *body*)
He's dead!

CYRANO

(*Aside, drawing his sword*)
And now I too must die, since, without knowing it, she's
mourning for me in him!

(*Trumpets in the distance.* DE GUICHE *reappears on the parapet, bareheaded, with a wound on his forehead.*)

DE GUICHE
(*In a thunderous voice*)
That's the signal! A fanfare! The French are on their way back to camp with provisions! Hold fast a little longer!

ROXANE
There's blood on his letter, and tears!

A VOICE
(*Shouting from the other side of the embankment*)
Surrender!

CADETS' VOICES
No!

RAGUENEAU
(*Who has climbed up on his carriage to watch the battle beyond the embankment*)
They're coming closer!

CYRANO
(*To* DE GUICHE, *pointing to* ROXANE)
Take her away! I'm going to charge!

ROXANE
(*Feebly, kissing the letter*)
His blood! His tears!

RAGUENEAU
(*Leaping down from the carriage and running toward her*)
She's fainted!

DE GUICHE
(*On the parapet, shouting fiercely to the* CADETS)
Hold fast!

A VOICE
(*From beyond the embankment*)
Lay down your arms!

CADETS' VOICES
No!

CYRANO
(*To* DE GUICHE)
You've proved your valor, sir. (*Points to* ROXANE.) Flee now, and save her!

DE GUICHE

(*Hurrying to* ROXANE *and picking her up in his arms*)
I'll do it, for her sake. But we can win if you gain time!

CYRANO

We will! (*Watches* ROXANE, *unconscious, being carried away by* DE GUICHE *and* RAGUENEAU.) Good-by, Roxane!
(*Tumult. Shouts.* CADETS *reappear, wounded, and fall onstage.* CYRANO, *rushing toward the battle, is stopped on the parapet by* CARBON, *covered with blood.*)

CARBON

We're giving ground! I've been wounded twice!

CYRANO

(*Shouting to the* CADETS *in their native Gascon tongue*)
Hardi! Reculès pas, drollos! (*To* CARBON, *holding him up*)
Don't give up hope! I have two deaths to avenge: Christian's and that of my happiness! (*They go downstage.* CYRANO *brandishes the lance to which* ROXANE's *handkerchief is tied.*) Float proudly, little lace banner bearing her monogram! (*Plants it on the parapet and again shouts to the* CADETS.) *Toumbé dèssus! Escrasas lous!* (*To the fifer*)
Play your fife!
(*The fifer plays. Some of the wounded men stand up. Other* CADETS *come down the embankment and group themselves around* CYRANO *and the little flag. The carriage is filled and covered with men. Bristling with muskets, it is transformed into a redoubt. A* CADET *appears on the parapet, moving backward, still fighting.*)

THE CADET

(*Shouting*)
They're coming up the embankment!
(*He falls dead.*)

CYRANO

We'll give them a salute!
(*In an instant the parapet is crowned by a formidable line of enemy soldiers. Large Imperial banners are raised.*)

CYRANO

Fire!
(*General volley*)

A VOICE

(*Shouting from the enemy ranks*)
Fire!
(*Murderous counterfire.* CADETS *fall on all sides.*)

A SPANISH OFFICER

Who are these men who have such scorn for death?

CYRANO

(*Reciting, facing the enemy fire*)
These are the stouthearted Gascon Cadets
Of Carbon de Castel-Jaloux;
They fight over trifles and shamelessly lie. . . .
(*He rushes forward, followed by the few survivors.*)
These are the stouthearted Gascon . . .
(*The rest is lost in the tumult of battle.*)

CURTAIN

ACT FIVE

Cyrano's Gazette

*Fifteen years later, in 1655. The park of the con-
vent occupied by the Ladies of the Cross, in Paris.*

*Magnificent, shady foliage. To the left, the house,
whose front steps lead up to a broad landing with
several doors opening onto it. An enormous tree in
the middle of the stage, standing alone in a small oval-
shaped open space. Downstage right, a semicircular
stone bench among large box shrubs.*

*A lane bordered by chestnut trees crosses the entire
background and ends at the door of a chapel on the
right, half hidden among the branches. Beyond the
lane, seen through the double row of chestnut trees,
are stretches of lawn, other lanes, groves, the depths of
the park, and the sky.*

*A side door of the chapel opens into a colonnade,
entwined by reddened vines, which vanishes behind the
box shrubs downstage right.*

*It is autumn. The foliage above the green lawn has
turned red. Spots of darker color formed by box shrubs
and yew trees that have remained green. A carpet of
yellow leaves under each tree. Dead leaves are strewn
over the whole stage; they crackle underfoot along the
lanes, and half cover the bench and the landing at the
top of the front steps.*

Between the bench on the right and the tree, a large embroidery frame with a small chair in front of it. Baskets full of skeins and balls of thread. A tapestry has been begun in the frame.

As the curtain rises, NUNS *are coming and going in the park. Some are seated on the bench, around an older* NUN. *Leaves are falling.*

Scene I

Mother Marguerite, Sister Marthe, Sister Claire, other Nuns.

SISTER MARTHE
(*To* MOTHER MARGUERITE)
Sister Claire has stopped in front of the mirror twice, to see how her headdress looks.

MOTHER MARGUERITE
(*To* SISTER CLAIRE)
That's odious.

SISTER CLAIRE
But Sister Marthe took a prune from the tart this morning. I saw her!

MOTHER MARGUERITE
(*To* SISTER MARTHE)
That's disgraceful, Sister Marthe.

SISTER CLAIRE
One little look!

SISTER MARTHE
One little prune!

MOTHER MARGUERITE
(*Sternly*)
I'll tell Monsieur Cyrano this evening.

SISTER CLAIRE
(*Alarmed*)
No! He'll make fun of us!

SISTER MARTHE
He'll say that nuns are very coquettish!

SISTER CLAIRE
And very greedy!

MOTHER MARGUERITE

(*Smiling*)

And very good.

SISTER CLAIRE

He's been coming every Saturday for the past ten years, hasn't he, Mother Marguerite de Jésus?

MOTHER MARGUERITE

Longer than that! Ever since his cousin came to us fourteen years ago, mingling her black mourning veil with our linen hoods, like a raven among a flock of white doves.

SISTER MARTHE

In all the time since she first took a room in this cloister, no one but Monsieur Cyrano has ever been able to distract her from the grief that afflicts her night and day.

ALL THE NUNS

He's so amusing!—His visits are delightful!—He teases us!—Such a nice man!—We all like him!—He always appreciates the pastry we make for him!

SISTER MARTHE

But he's not a very good Catholic!

SISTER CLAIRE

We'll convert him.

OTHER NUNS

Yes! Yes!

MOTHER MARGUERITE

I forbid you to make any efforts in that direction, my children. Don't torment him: he might come less often!

SISTER MARTHE

But God . . .

MOTHER MARGUERITE

Have no fear: I'm sure God knows him well.

SISTER MARTHE

But when he comes in every Saturday he says to me proudly, "Sister, I ate meat yesterday!"

MOTHER MARGUERITE

Oh? Is that what he tells you? Well, the last time he came, he hadn't eaten anything for two days.

SISTER MARTHE

Oh, Mother!

MOTHER MARGUERITE

He's poor.

SISTER MARTHE

Who told you so?

MOTHER MARGUERITE

Monsieur Le Bret.

SISTER MARTHE

Doesn't anyone help him?

MOTHER MARGUERITE

No. It would only make him angry if anyone tried. (ROXANE *appears, walking slowly along a lane in the background. She is dressed in black, with a widow's cap and long veils.* DE GUICHE, *who has aged gracefully, walks beside her.* MOTHER MARGUERITE *stands up.*) Come, we must go inside. Madame Magdeleine is strolling in the park with a visitor.

SISTER MARTHE

(*Softly, to* SISTER CLAIRE)
It's the Marshal Duke de Grammont, isn't it?

SISTER CLAIRE

(*Looking*)
Yes, I think so.

SISTER MARTHE

This is the first time he's come to see her for months!

OTHER NUNS

He's very busy.—The court.—The army. . . .

SISTER CLAIRE

Worldly concerns!
(*The* NUNS *leave.* DE GUICHE *and* ROXANE *come downstage in silence and stop near the embroidery frame. Several moments pass.*)

Scene II

Roxane, the Duke de Grammont (formerly Count de Guiche), then Le Bret and Ragueneau.

THE DUKE

And so you remain here, letting your blond beauty go to waste, still in mourning?

ROXANE

Still in mourning.

THE DUKE

And still faithful?

ROXANE

Still faithful.

THE DUKE
(*After a moment of silence*)
Have you forgiven me?

ROXANE
(*Simply, looking at the cross of the convent*)
Of course, since I'm here.
(*Another silence.*)

THE DUKE

Was he really such a . . .

ROXANE

He showed his true nature only to those who knew him
well.

THE DUKE

His true nature? . . . Yes, perhaps I didn't know him well
enough. . . . Do you still carry his last letter over your
heart?

ROXANE

Yes, like a holy relic.

THE DUKE

You love him even in death?

ROXANE

Sometimes it seems to me that he's not really dead. I feel
that our hearts are together, and that his love floats around
me, very much alive!

THE DUKE
(*After another silence*)
Does Cyrano come to see you?

ROXANE

Yes, often. My old friend gives me all the news; he re-
places the gazettes for me. He visits me regularly. If the
weather is good, his chair is always brought out and placed
under this tree. I embroider while I wait for him. When the
clock strikes the hour of his arrival, I don't even turn
around to look for him, because I know I'll hear his cane
coming down the steps immediately after the last stroke.
He sits down and laughs at my eternal tapestry. Then he
begins telling me about the week's happenings, and . . .

(LE BRET *appears on the steps.*) Ah! Here's Le Bret! (LE BRET *comes down.*) How is our friend doing?

LE BRET

Badly.

THE DUKE

Oh!

ROXANE

(*To the* DUKE)
He's exaggerating!

LE BRET

Cyrano is living in isolation and poverty, just as I predicted! His writings constantly make new enemies for him! He attacks false noblemen, false saints, false heroes, plagiarists— everyone!

ROXANE

But his sword fills everyone with terror. No one will ever get the best of him.

THE DUKE

(*Shaking his head*)
Who knows?

LE BRET

I'm not afraid of his meeting a violent death. Loneliness, hunger, the cold of winter creeping into his dark room— those are the assassins that will end his life! He tightens his belt one more notch every day, his poor nose has turned as pale as ivory, he has only one threadbare black coat. . . .

THE DUKE

It's certainly true that he hasn't scaled the heights of worldly success, but don't feel too sorry for him.

LE BRET

(*With a bitter smile*)
Sir, you . . .

THE DUKE

No, don't feel too sorry for him: he lives without compromise, free in both his thoughts and his acts.

LE BRET

(*Still smiling bitterly*)
Sir, you . . .

THE DUKE

(*Loftily*)
Yes, I know: I have everything and he has nothing. But I'd

be honored to shake his hand. (*Bows to* ROXANE.) I must
go. Good-by.

ROXANE

I'll accompany you to the door.
(*The* DUKE *bows to* LE BRET *and walks toward the steps
with* ROXANE.)

THE DUKE

(*Stopping as they are climbing the steps*)
Yes, sometimes I envy him. When a man has been too
successful in life, even though he hasn't done anything
really wrong, he still has all sorts of reasons for feeling a
little disgusted with himself. Their combined weight isn't
enough to form a burden of remorse, but he can never
escape a kind of vague uneasiness. As he continues to
climb toward even greater success, he hears dead illusions
and old regrets rustling under his ducal mantle, like the
fallen leaves swept along by the train of your black dress
when you mount these steps.

ROXANE

(*Ironically*)
You're in a thoughtful mood today.

THE DUKE

Yes, I'm afraid so. (*Abruptly, just as he is about to leave*)
Monsieur Le Bret! (*To* ROXANE) Will you excuse me? I
want to have a word with him. (*Goes to* LE BRET *and
speaks in a low voice.*) It's true that no one would dare to
attack our friend openly, but it's also true that he's hated
by many people. Only yesterday, during a card game at
court, someone said to me, "That Cyrano may have a fatal
accident someday."

LE BRET

Oh?

THE DUKE

Yes. Tell him not to go out very often, and to be careful.

LE BRET

(*Throwing up his arms*)
Careful! . . . He'll soon be here; I'll warn him. But . . .

ROXANE

(*Who has remained on the steps, to a* NUN *coming
toward her*)
What is it?

THE NUN

Ragueneau would like to see you, madame.

ROXANE

Bring him in. (*To the* DUKE *and* LE BRET) He's come to
complain about his poverty. Since the day when he set out
to be a writer, he's been a singer . . .

LE BRET

A bathhouse attendant . . .

ROXANE

An actor . . .

LE BRET

A beadle . . .

ROXANE

A hairdresser . . .

LE BRET

A lute teacher . . .

ROXANE

What can he have become now?

RAGUENEAU

(*Entering rapidly*)
Ah, madame! (*Sees* LE BRET.) Sir!

ROXANE

(*Smiling*)
Tell Le Bret your troubles. I'll be back soon.

RAGUENEAU

But madame . . .
(ROXANE *ignores him and leaves with the* DUKE. RAGUE-
NEAU *goes to* LE BRET.)

Scene III

Le Bret, Ragueneau.

RAGUENEAU

Since you're here, I'd rather she didn't know. . . . As I was
approaching our friend's house this afternoon, on my way
to visit him, I saw him come out. I hurried to catch up with
him. I can't say for certain that it wasn't an accident, but
when he was about to turn the corner a lackey dropped a
piece of firewood on him from an upstairs window.

LE BRET

The cowards! . . . Cyrano! . . .

RAGUENEAU

I ran to him. . , .

LE BRET

It's horrible!

RAGUENEAU

Our friend, sir, our poet, was lying on the ground with a big hole in his head!

LE BRET

Is he dead?

RAGUENEAU

No, but . . . My God! . . . I carried him back into his house, to his room, rather. Oh, that room! What a wretched little closet!

LE BRET

Is he in pain?

RAGUENEAU

No, sir, he's unconscious.

LE BRET

Did you bring a doctor?

RAGUENEAU

Yes, I found one who was willing to come out of charity.

LE BRET

Poor Cyrano! . . . We mustn't tell Roxane all at once. . . . What did the doctor say?

RAGUENEAU

I don't remember very clearly, something about fever, and the meninges. . . . Oh, if you'd seen him lying there, with his head wrapped in bandages! . . . Come with me quickly! There's no one with him now, and he may die if he tries to get up!

LE BRET

(*Leading him to the right*)

Let's go this way, through the chapel. It's shorter.

(ROXANE *appears on the steps and sees* LE BRET *hurrying along the colonnade that leads to the side door of the chapel.*)

ROXANE

Monsieur Le Bret! (LE BRET *and* RAGUENEAU *leave without*

answering.) Le Bret runs away when I call him? Poor Ragueneau must really be in trouble this time!
(*She comes down the steps.*)

Scene IV

Roxane, alone; then two Nuns, briefly.

ROXANE
What a beautiful autumn day! Even my sorrow is smiling. It's offended by April, but gives in to the gentler charm of September. (*She sits down in front of her embroidery frame. Two* NUNS *come out of the house, carrying a large armchair, and set it down under a tree.*) Ah, here's the chair for my old friend!

SISTER MARTHE
It's the best one in the visiting room!

ROXANE
Thank you, Sister. (*The* NUNS *leave.*) He'll soon be here. (*She begins working. The clock strikes.*) There, it's time. I'll take out my skeins. . . . This is surprising: the clock has finished striking and he's not here yet. Is he going to be late for the first time? The Sister at the door must be—Where's my thimble? There, I see it—must be trying to persuade him to repent of his sins. (*Several moments pass.*) Still persuading him! He'll surely be here before long. . . . A dead leaf. . . . (*She brushes aside the leaf that has fallen onto the embroidery frame.*) Nothing could—My scissors . . . in my bag!—prevent him from coming!

A NUN
(*Appearing on the steps*)
Monsieur de Bergerac is here.

Scene V

Roxane, Cyrano, and briefly, Sister Marthe.

ROXANE
(*Without turning around*)
I knew it! (*She continues her work.* CYRANO *appears. He is*

very pale, and his hat is pulled down over his eyes. The NUN *who has accompanied him leaves. He slowly comes down the steps, leaning on his cane and making an obvious effort to stay on his feet.* ROXANE *is still working.*) Oh, these faded colors! . . . How will I ever match them? (*To* CYRANO, *in a tone of friendly rebuke*) Late, for the first time in fourteen years!

(CYRANO *has succeeded in reaching his chair and sitting down in it. When he speaks, his cheerful voice contrasts with his face.*)

CYRANO

Yes, it's scandalous! I can't tell you how annoyed I am. I was delayed by . . .

ROXANE

By what?

CYRANO

By an untimely visit.

ROXANE
(*Distractedly, still working*)
A friend of yours?

CYRANO

An old acquaintance. We've met on the battlefield, among other places. I knew we'd meet again some day, but this wasn't the time for it.

ROXANE

You sent him away?

CYRANO

Yes, I said to him, "Excuse me, but this is Saturday, the day when I always keep a certain appointment. Nothing can make me miss it. Come back in an hour."

ROXANE
(*Lightly*)
Well, I'm afraid he'll have to wait for you, because I won't let you leave before nightfall.

CYRANO
(*Gently*)
I may have to leave a little sooner than that.
(*He closes his eyes and remains silent.* SISTER MARTHE *walks across the park, from the chapel to the steps.* ROXANE *sees her and nods to her.*)

ROXANE

(*To* CYRANO)
Aren't you going to tease Sister Marthe today?

CYRANO

(*Quickly, opening his eyes*)
Yes, of course! (*In a comically gruff voice*) Sister Marthe!
Come here! (*She comes to him.*) When you have such
lovely eyes, why do you keep them cast down?

SISTER MARTHE

(*Looking up with a smile*)
I . . . (*Sees his face and makes a gesture of astonishment.*)
Oh!

CYRANO

(*In an undertone, pointing to* ROXANE)
Sh! It's nothing. . . . (*Loudly and truculently*) I ate meat
yesterday!

SISTER MARTHE

I know. (*Aside*) He's pale from hunger! (*Rapidly, in a low
voice*) Come to the dining hall in a little while and I'll
give you a big bowl of soup. Will you come?

CYRANO

Yes, yes, yes.

SISTER MARTHE

Ah, you're a little more sensible today!

ROXANE

(*Who has heard them whispering*)
She's trying to convert you!

SISTER MARTHE

I'm doing no such thing!

CYRANO

Now that I think of it, you're always full of pious platitudes,
yet you never preach to me! It's amazing! (*With mock
ferocity*) I'll show you that you're not the only one who
can be amazing! Just listen to this! I'm going to . . . (*Seems
to be trying to think of a good way to tease her.*) Ah! I've
got it! I'm going to allow you to pray for me tonight in the
chapel!

ROXANE

Oh! Oh!

CYRANO

(*Laughing*)
Sister Marthe is dumbfounded!

SISTER MARTHE

(*Gently*)
I haven't waited for your permission.
(*She goes into the house.*)

CYRANO

(*Turning back to* ROXANE, *who is leaning over her work*)
May the devil take me if I ever see that tapestry finished!

ROXANE

I was expecting some such remark.
(*A breeze makes some leaves fall.*)

CYRANO

The leaves . . .

ROXANE

(*Raising her head and looking into the distance*)
They're Titian red. . . . Look at them falling.

CYRANO

How well they fall! Such beauty in that short drop from
branch to earth! Despite their terror of rotting on the
ground, they give their fall the grace of flight.

ROXANE

Can it be that you're melancholy—you?

CYRANO

(*Catching himself*)
Not at all!

ROXANE

Then forget about the falling leaves and tell me the latest
news. Aren't you still my gazette?

CYRANO

I'll begin this very moment.

ROXANE

Good.

CYRANO

(*More and more pale, struggling against his pain*)
Last Saturday, the nineteenth, after eating eight helpings of
preserved fruit, the King took to his bed with a fever; his
illness was convicted of high treason and executed by his
physician, and since then the royal pulse has returned to
normal. At the Queen's ball on Sunday, seven hundred and
sixty-three white wax candles were burned. Our troops are
reported to have beaten John of Austria.* Four sorcerers

* John of Austria (1629–1679), Spanish general defeated by the
French in Flanders.

have been hanged. Madame d'Athis's little dog had to be given an enema to . . .

ROXANE

That will do, Monsieur de Bergerac!

CYRANO

On Monday . . . nothing. Lygdamire took a new lover.

ROXANE

Oh!

CYRANO

(*Whose face is increasingly twisted by pain*)
On Tuesday, the whole court went to Fontainebleau. On Wednesday, Madame Montglat said no to Count de Fiesque. On Thursday, Olympe Mancini* was the Queen of France —or almost! On Friday, the twenty-fifth, Madame Montglat said yes to Count de Fiesque. And today, Saturday the twenty-sixth . . .
  (*He closes his eyes and his head falls. Silence. Surprised at no longer hearing him speak,* ROXANE *turns and looks at him, then stands up in alarm.*)

ROXANE

Has he fainted? (*Hurries to him with a cry.*) Cyrano!

CYRANO

(*Vaguely, opening his eyes*)
What is it? . . . What . . . (*Seeing her leaning over him, he quickly puts his hand to his hat to make sure it is still pulled down, and draws away from her in his chair.*) No! It's nothing, believe me! Go back to your chair.

ROXANE

But you . . .

CYRANO

It's only my old wound from Arras. Sometimes it . . . You know. . . .

ROXANE

My poor friend!

CYRANO

It's really nothing. It will soon go away. (*Smiles with an effort.*) There, it's gone.

ROXANE

(*Standing beside him*)
Each of us has his wound. Mine is old but still unhealed,

---

* Olympe Mancini (1639–1708), one of Louis XIV's mistresses, who briefly had hopes of marrying him.

here . . . (*Puts her hand to her bosom.*) . . . under the yellowed paper of a letter still stained with tears and blood!
(*Twilight is beginning to fall.*)

CYRANO

His letter! . . . Didn't you once tell me that you might let me read it some day?

ROXANE

You want to read . . . his letter?

CYRANO

Yes, I do. Now.

ROXANE

(*Removing the little bag that hangs from around her neck*)
Here!

CYRANO

(*Taking it*)
May I open it?

ROXANE

Yes, read it.
(*She goes back to the embroidery frame and begins putting away her thread.*)

CYRANO

(*Reading*)
"Farewell, Roxane! Death is near. . . ."

ROXANE

(*Stopping in surprise*)
You're reading it aloud?

CYRANO

(*Reading*)
"I believe this will be my last day, my beloved. My soul is still heavy with unexpressed love, and I must die! Never again will my eyes delight . . ."

ROXANE

How well you read his letter!

CYRANO

(*Continuing*)
". . . will my eyes delight in kissing each of your graceful gestures. I remember one of them, a way of putting your hand to your forehead, and I want to cry out . . ."

ROXANE

(*Troubled*)
How well you read ... that letter!
(*The twilight is turning to darkness.*)

CYRANO

"... to cry out, 'Good-by!' ..."

ROXANE

You read it ...

CYRANO

"... my dearest, my darling, my treasure ..."

ROXANE

(*Thoughtfully*)
... in a voice that ...

CYRANO

"... my love!"

ROXANE

... that ... (*She starts.*) A voice that I'm not hearing for
the first time!
(*She slowly approaches him without his seeing her, stands
behind his chair, silently bends down, and looks at the
letter. The darkness is deepening.*)

CYRANO

"My heart has never left you for a moment, and in the next
world my love for you will still be as boundless, as ..."

ROXANE

(*Putting her hand on his shoulder*)
How can you read now? It's dark. (*He starts, turns around,
sees her standing close to him, makes a gesture of alarm,
and bows his head. A long silence. Then, in the shadowy
darkness, she clasps her hands and speaks slowly.*) And for
fourteen years you played the part of an old friend who
came to be amusing!

CYRANO

Roxane!

ROXANE

It was you.

CYRANO

No, Roxane, no!

ROXANE

I should have guessed it each time I heard you say my
name!

CYRANO

No! It wasn't . . .

ROXANE

It *was* you!

CYRANO

I swear . . .

ROXANE

I see the whole selfless imposture now! The letters . . . It
was you.

CYRANO

No!

ROXANE

The wild, endearing words . . . It was you.

CYRANO

No!

ROXANE

The voice in the night . . . It was you.

CYRANO

I swear it wasn't!

ROXANE

The soul . . . It was yours!

CYRANO

I didn't love you!

ROXANE

You did love me!

CYRANO

(*Desperately*)
It was Christian!

ROXANE

You loved me!

CYRANO

(*In a weakening voice*)
No!

ROXANE

You already deny it less strongly!

CYRANO

No, no, my love, I didn't love you!

ROXANE

Ah, how many things have died, and how many have now

been born! Why were you silent for fourteen years, knowing that he hadn't written that letter, and that the tears on it were yours?

CYRANO

(*Handing her the letter*)
The blood was his.

ROXANE

And why have you let that sublime silence be broken this evening?

CYRANO

Why? . . .
(LE BRET *and* RAGUENEAU *enter, running*.)

Scene VI

Cyrano, Roxane, Le Bret, Ragueneau.

LE BRET

What foolhardiness! I knew we'd find him here!

CYRANO

(*Smiling, and sitting more erect*)
You were right. Here I am.

LE BRET

(*To* ROXANE)
He's killed himself by leaving his bed!

ROXANE

Oh, God! . . . (*To* CYRANO) Your faintness a little while ago . . . Was it . . .

CYRANO

That reminds me: I didn't finish my gazette! Today, Saturday the twenty-sixth, an hour before dinner time, Monsieur de Bergerac was murdered.
(*He takes off his hat, showing the bandages around his head.*)

ROXANE

What is he saying? . . . Cyrano! . . . Those bandages! . . . What have they done to you? Why?

CYRANO

"To be struck down by the only noble weapon, the sword, wielded by an adversary worthy of me . . ." Yes, I once said that. Fate is a great jester! I've been struck down, but from behind, in an ambush, by a lackey wielding a log! I've been consistent to the end. I've failed in everything, even in my death.

RAGUENEAU

Oh, sir! . . .

CYRANO

Don't weep so loudly, Ragueneau. (*Takes his hand.*) Tell me, brother poet, what are you doing these days?

RAGUENEAU

(*Through his tears*)
I'm the candle-snuffer in a theater . . . Molière's* company. . . .

CYRANO

Molière!

RAGUENEAU

Yes, but I'm leaving him tomorrow. I'm outraged! Yesterday they played his *Scapin,* and I saw that he'd taken a scene from you!

LE BRET

A whole scene!

RAGUENEAU

Yes, sir, the famous "What the devil was he doing? . . ."

LE BRET

(*Furious*)
Molière took it from you!

CYRANO

Be calm. He was right to take it. (*To* RAGUENEAU) How did the audience react to the scene?

RAGUENEAU

(*Sobbing*)
Oh, sir, they laughed and laughed!

CYRANO

Yes, my life has been that of a man who provides words and ideas for others, spurs them to action, and is then forgotten. (*To* ROXANE) Do you remember the evening when Christian spoke to you below your balcony? Well, that evening was the essence of my life: while I remained below, in

* Molière (1622–1673, real name Jean-Baptiste Poquelin), the great French comic playwright, had his own theatrical company, for which he wrote his plays.

the shadows, others climbed up to receive the kiss of glory. But now, on the threshold of my grave, I acknowledge the justice of it all—Molière is a genius, and Christian was handsome! (*The chapel bell has begun ringing; the* NUNS *are now seen walking along the lane in the background, on their way to Vespers.*) Let them go to their prayers, since their bell is ringing.

ROXANE
(*Looking up and calling*)
Sister! Sister!

CYRANO
(*Holding her back*)
No, no, don't go to bring anyone! You'd find me gone when you returned. (*The* NUNS *have entered the chapel, and the organ is heard.*) I needed a little harmony, and there it is.

ROXANE
I love you! You must live!

CYRANO
No. In the fairy tale, when Beauty said, "I love you" to the prince, his ugliness melted away like snow in the warmth of the sun, but as you can see, those words have no such magic effect on me.

ROXANE
Your life has been unhappy because of me! Me!

CYRANO
No, Roxane, quite the contrary. Feminine sweetness was unknown to me. My mother made it clear that she didn't find me pleasant to look at. I had no sister. Later, I dreaded the thought of seeing mockery in the eyes of a mistress. Thanks to you, I've at least had a woman's friendship, a gracious presence to soften the harsh loneliness of my life.

LE BRET
(*Pointing to the moonlight shining through the branches*)
Your other friend has come to visit you.

CYRANO
(*Smiling at the moon*)
Yes, I see her.

ROXANE
I've loved only one man, and I've lost him twice!

CYRANO
Le Bret, I'll soon be soaring up to the moon, this time without having to invent a machine. . . .

ROXANE

The moon?

CYRANO

Yes, of course, that's where I'll be sent to find my paradise.
More than one soul that I love must be exiled there. I'll
be with Socrates, Galileo. . . .

LE BRET

(*Rebelling*)
No! No! A man like you, a poet with such a great and
noble heart—you can't die this way! It's too stupid! Too
unjust!

CYRANO

There's Le Bret—always complaining!

LE BRET

(*Bursting into tears*)
My dear friend . . .

CYRANO

(*Half raising himself from his chair, with a distraught
look in his eyes*)
These are the stouthearted Gascon Cadets. . . . The ele-
mental mass . . . Ah, yes . . . There's the difficulty. . . .

LE BRET

His learning stays with him, even in his delirium.

CYRANO

Copernicus said . . .

ROXANE

Oh!

CYRANO

But what the devil was he . . . what the devil was he doing
there? . . . "Philosopher, scientist, poet, swordsman, musician, aerial traveler, maker of sharp retorts, and lover (not
to his advantage!), here lies Savinien de Cyrano de Bergerac, who was everything, and who was nothing." Excuse
me, I must go now: a moonbeam has come to take me
away, and I can't keep it waiting! (*He falls back into his
chair.* ROXANE's *weeping recalls him to reality. He looks at
her and strokes her veils.*) I don't want you to mourn any
less for that good, charming, handsome Christian; my only
hope is that when the great cold has seeped into my bones,
you'll give a double meaning to those black veils, and
mourn for me a little when you mourn for him.

ROXANE

I swear to you that . . .
   (CYRANO *is shaken by a great tremor, and abruptly stands up.*)

CYRANO

No! Not there! Not in a chair! (*The others move toward him.*) Stand back! I want no support from anyone! (*Leans against the tree.*) Only from this tree! (*Silence*) He's coming. I already feel stone boots . . . lead gloves. . . . (*Stiffens himself.*) Yes, he's coming, but I'll meet him on my feet . . . (*Draws his sword.*) . . . sword in hand!

LE BRET

Cyrano!

ROXANE

   (*Half fainting*)
Cyrano!
   (*They all draw back in terror.*)

CYRANO

I believe I see . . . yes, I see him, with his noseless face, daring to look at my nose! (*Raises his sword.*) What's that you say? It's useless? Of course, but I've never needed hope of victory to make me fight! The noblest battles are always fought in vain! . . . You there, all of you, who are you? Your numbers seem endless. . . . Ah, I recognize you now: my old enemies! Lies! My greetings to you! (*Thrusts his sword into the empty air.*) And here's Compromise! And Prejudice! And Cowardice! (*Thrusts again.*) What's that? Come to terms with you? Never! Never! . . . Ah, there you are, Stupidity! . . . I know I can't defeat you all, I know that in the end you'll overwhelm me, but I'll still fight you as long as there's a breath in my body! (*Swings his sword in great arcs, then stops, panting.*) Yes, you've robbed me of everything: the laurels of glory, the roses of love! But there's one thing you can't take away from me. When I go to meet God this evening, and doff my hat before the holy gates, my salute will sweep the blue threshold of heaven, because I'll still have one thing intact, without a stain, something that I'll take with me in spite of you! (*Springs forward with his sword raised.*) You ask what it is? I'll tell you! It's . . .
   (*His sword drops from his hand; he staggers and falls into the arms of* LE BRET *and* RAGUENEAU.)

ROXANE
(*Bending down and kissing him on the forehead*)
What is it?

CYRANO
(*Opening his eyes and smiling at her*)
My white plume.

CURTAIN

For your reading pleasure...